GOD'S QUESTIONS

GOD'S QUESTIONS:
Vision, Strategy and Growth

Peter Brierley

Publishers

First published 2010 by ADBC Publishers
1 Thorpe Avenue, Tonbridge, Kent TN10 4PW, UK

British Library Cataloguing in Publication Data
A catalogue record for this book is available from the British Library

ISBN-13: 978-0-9566577-0-1

Cover design by David McNeill
Printed and bound in the UK by Bell & Bain Ltd., Glasgow

To my wife Cherry, ill for many years, but whose continued encouragement, help and dogged determination to keep on keeping on has been a huge inspiration both to me and many others.

CONTENTS

FOREWORD

Peter Brierley's work hardly needs either introduction or commendation from me. His reputation goes before him as a perceptive analyst of statistical trends, and a trustworthy interpreter of their meaning for churches and their leaders. In 1983, Peter became director of MARC Europe, which was the same year that I was invited to become convener of the mission committee of the Scottish Churches Council. From different starting points we have both been concerned to offer a new vision for the church in the twenty-first century that will be contextually appropriate, while also being deeply rooted in the ancient tradition.

I just love the title of this book – not least because it follows the example of Jesus, who regularly taught by asking questions. At a time when so many voices offer slick answers to the challenges facing the church in today's ever-changing culture, the truly prophetic individuals are those who know how to formulate the right questions. Peter Brierley is one of those, and in these chapters readers will find many words of wisdom on matters as varied as pastoral care and strategic vision (and, of course, statistics). This is not just a book of theories, though, because underlying it all is a profound understanding of people and the ways in which we operate in our personal lives as well as our professional contexts. Inevitably, many challenges are presented, but always in a context of encouragement, and underlying everything is a conviction that the lessons of the Bible are as relevant now as when its books were first penned, and that God is no less active in today's world than in the past.

There is ample evidence here of wide reading of current research that goes well beyond Peter's own primary field of statistics. But it is all illustrated by the use of down-to-earth examples drawn from Peter's own life and the spiritual journeys of others he has worked with over the years. This is someone who understands the realities of church life, and each chapter offers practical techniques for dealing with everything from determining major life priorities to making decisions about what to do next this afternoon. It is, quite simply, the fruit of a lifetime of reflection on God, faith, church and culture.

John Drane
Professor of Practical Theology
University of Aberdeen

SECTION 1
THE FIVE QUESTIONS

Introduction:

WHAT IS THIS?

Above my desk at home is a picture made up of 15 different photographs, all overlapping each other, in a montage taken when I had climbed a small hill in one of the beautiful Scottish valleys overlooking a loch. From that vantage point I could see a huge distance, more than one tier of hills, and rolling vistas of sky, water, grass and trees. To use other language, it is 'the big picture'. From the questions I am asked in my ministry it seems that some leaders in our churches, lay or ordained, simply don't see the big picture – and this is stated not as a criticism, but just a fact.

One leader is always at his desk at 8 a.m. every morning beginning to answer his post and emails. Then the phone rings – someone is ill, can he come? Then there is a knock on the door – has he got the spare key to the boiler room? And he knows he must prepare somehow for that 10.30 meeting. In the hurly burly of life, how do you retain your focus?

'Should we cater for a different group of people by starting another service or another congregation?' someone asked. Before the minister could reply, one regular attender butted in, 'Well, that depends on where the church is going.' Where is your church going, and how is it going to get there? Mission Action Plans are very commendable, but how well do they work in practice?

One minister was caught by a recently retired domineering member of her congregation who insisted that the way forward was for detailed reports to be written about each section of the church's current work for further discussion by the leadership. The minister knew this was not the answer but couldn't bring herself to say so. Instead, the retiree won the day, and a process was begun that took all the church's energies for the next 3 years. The minister didn't know how to be strong and assertive enough with such individuals.

He knew that a long hike in the Peak District would help clear his thoughts. It was a wonderful day and the rugged hills inspired him, and he had a super meal at the village pub. What did he have to change to help things move forward? Now he knew, and the problem became less one of identification of actions to one of resolution of will to make it happen.

• • • • • • •

These are just some of the situations that are frequently experienced in church life: (a) identifying where you are in the overall picture of church life; (b) knowing your priorities and how to implement them; (c) resolving your church's vision and the strategy to make it happen; (d) understanding enough about yourself as a leader to know what you should and can do, and what to avoid; and (e) having the faith to believe that things can change and with it the confidence to start making the invisible visible. That is what this book is about – one chapter for each topic, and two further chapters to put these five in their context – in the hope that thereby some leaders may become stronger and more effective in their service.

Martin Luther is supposed to have said, 'I only have two days on my calendar – today and that day.' The present and the future – these chapters are intended to be about the present so that you may do the future better.

1

WHERE ARE YOU?

This is a *haunting* question. It is the first question that God asks in the Bible. It is put to Adam who had sinned by eating fruit from the forbidden tree of the knowledge of good and evil in the Garden of Eden. Adam was attempting to hide from God because he knew he was naked, a realization which had only come about after eating the fruit. God, of course, knew where Adam was. Furthermore, if you'd asked Adam, he knew that God knew where he was. You can't hide from God. All our ways are open to him. Nevertheless, the question, 'Where are you?'(Gen. 3:9) is a relevant, searching one, which, in our need for strategic ways forward, is an excellent place to start. If we do not know where we are, we cannot easily move forward.

There is a complementary factor to the question also. Adam had to face up to its answer. He was where he was because he was trying to hide, shamed at the consequences of his sin. This question should help us, too, to face up to reality. 'Our church is growing,' we may proclaim. Good news! How many people have found faith through the ministry of your church as opposed to transferring from another church or moving into your district? The impression we want to give to others may not truly be where we are. Not every Christian family is a happy family – can we face up to this? Not every child in a churchgoing family goes to church – can we look at why that may be? Not every leader is as secure as they like to show – is there an inner honesty about personal depression and frustration? The question 'Where are you?' therefore carries a corollary. Having found an answer, are you willing to move from that position? If the answer to that is positive, then this book is for you.

The external context

There are at least three aspects to the question 'Where are you?'. The first is the external context – where is your church in relation to other churches in your neighbourhood, or to your denomination or to churches about your size (bringing in area and peer evaluations)? Adam was in Eden, and, it would seem from Genesis 3:13 where God speaks to Eve, his wife Eve was with him. Are there others with you in similar situations? At one Vision Building Day I was asked to lead, we looked at all six Anglican churches in a particular town centre – acknowledging their differences, but also focusing on what they had in common.

Where is your agency with respect to others in your neighbourhood, or to others undertaking similar work to your own, or to others of about the same size as yours? Is your church or organization doing as well as, or better than, others in your area or of similar size? Is your budget about the same for the number of people you have or donors or customers you serve? Is the number of staff or volunteers the same proportion of the total attendance or customer base as others doing similar work? There is a host of such questions which may be asked or ratios to be evaluated: the purpose of which is to find out how similar you are to others (in which case you might face similar opportunities and problems) or in what ways you are different.

If you are different, how can you best use your strengths, and how can you try and overcome your weaknesses? This kind of contextual evaluation is crucial if you are determined to find out where you are. You can't win a game of snakes and ladders if you don't know which square your counter is on! This aspect of context-ualization is so important that we will devote chapter 6 to this one facet of enquiry.

That leaves two other aspects – the corporate aspect and the individual aspect. Both are equally important, and if one is out of phase with the other ('I don't really agree with where this organization is going') then considerable disquiet and disharmony can result. These two aspects are considered in this chapter. (If you are reading primarily from a personal viewpoint, you may wish to omit this.)

The corporate context

Looking at ourselves as a church or a Christian (or secular) agency frequently involves asking two types of questions: quantitative and qualitative. The minister of a certain church sent me an email – could I lead a day for his church leadership to help them think about ways forward for the church? I answered positively but there was a lot we could work out in advance. What is working for him in his church? What is not working? How many people come on a Sunday? Are there mid-week services? Roughly what proportions are in which age group? What youth activities, if any, does the church run? Approximately what proportion of those coming is male? The answers to these questions give a clue about the church. Only 27% of churches, for example, have mid-week youth activities; if this church is one of them, then there is a good chance it can move forward in the days to come. If it hasn't, then one of the outcomes of the day may well be to stress the importance of developing something especially for young people.

Before starting to answer such specific questions, however, there is a need to pause and think about another key aspect of institutional life which can be easily overlooked. 'Where are you?' assumes you have already started and presumably know where you are aiming to go. The question is therefore relative and a prior question, 'Why do you exist?', may have to be asked first. This is not so easy, even if it may be written in the Articles of Association or Trust Deed, as it needs to be answered by the present minister or chief executive. For example, I was the founding Executive Director of an organization called Christian Research which existed in my understanding as seeking 'to strengthen church leadership' albeit through research but in other ways also. When I retired my successor, Benita Hewitt, probably preferred to say that the organization existed 'to undertake research'. This may seem simply to be playing with semantics, but the consequence is that when answering the question 'Where are you?' I would have answered in terms of the number of leaders coming to seminars and conferences whereas my successor answers in terms of research projects completed or under way. Both types of answer are correct, because they spring from different replies to the basic issue – why do you exist?

Why do you exist?

In a previous book looking at vision formulation, this was described as 'What is your purpose?'.[1] However, this question is clearer and crisper. Walt Disney gives a short answer to such a question: 'To make people happy'; whether we agree depends perhaps on our experience of DisneyWorld or our enjoyment of some of the films, but at least we know what they are trying to do. The pharmaceutical firm Merck express the reason they are here (why they exist) as 'To preserve and improve human life' which suggests a high moral purpose.

Likewise, church leaders can give quite different types of answer to the questions 'Why is your church here?' or 'Why does your (local) church exist?'. These are the actual statements of different church leaders, and it will be obvious that their answers to the subsequent question 'Where are you?' will vary considerably.

'To meet the spiritual needs of the people in our parish (or local area).' *Roman Catholic priest, Tyneside.*

'To be a place where social, spiritual and community needs are met in an atmosphere of Christian love.' *United Reformed Church minister, North London.*

'To reach out in evangelism and service.' *Anglican minister, the Midlands.*

'To establish a presence in a Muslim area.' *Church leader, a northern English town.*

'To fulfil a need on a new estate.' *Church of Scotland minister, Livingston.*

The question 'Why do you exist?' was asked of some Anglican church leaders at a seminar in Kenya, and their replies, again quoting their actual words, immediately show they are reflecting a very different culture.[2]

'To reach out in evangelism.'

'To ease administration.'

'To resolve conflict.'

'To provide a church closer for elderly people.' [As all have to walk to church.]

'To deal with church politics.'

So, please pause for a moment. Why does your church, your parish, your agency exist? Why are you here? You may have noticed that all of the illustrations given start with an infinitive, and you may find it easier to answer the question if you do the same:

My church / agency [delete one] exists 'to_____

_____

_____

Where are you?

This is the follow-on question, to be answered in the light of why you exist. If you answered as one Kenyan church leader did 'To reach out in evangelism', then how many people have you seen converted or coming to faith in, say, the last 12 months? As Adam found, we have to face up to our present situation. Our dreams may be great, but we have to face reality, exploring it slightly differently for a church or an organization.

Essential questions for a church

The following questions may be relevant in this context: it is worth writing down your answers (and dating them for future reference), so that they can be shared with others. They could also be the basis of a discussion between several leaders, in which case it is worth keeping a note of the outcome.

1 How many people have started coming to your church in the last year? Have they joined because they came to faith, moved into your area, were born into a church family, transferred from another church, are immigrants joining friends or family, or another reason?

2 How many people have stopped coming to your church in the last 12 months? Did they leave because they moved away, lost their faith, transferred to another church, died, or for another reason?

3 How old are the people who attend, and what is their gender? What proportion is under 15, or 65 and over? How do these proportions compare with people in your neighbourhood (that is, the general population), or with other churches in your area, your church-manship, your denomination or environment?[3]

4 How are you involved with your local community? How many mid-week meetings does your church hold which non-regular churchgoers attend? What is your church known for? If you walked incognito down the High Street and got talking with someone and you mentioned you went to St Mary's, and they said, 'Oh yes, that's the church which . . .' how would they end the sentence?

5 How deep is the spiritual life of the church? If your congregation could score it out of 10 (1 low, 10 high), what mark would they give it? What mark would you give it? What mark would your bishop, superintendent, regional minister or senior advisor give it? You may want to answer this question first – how do you measure the depth of the spiritual life of a church?

6 What do you wish you were doing? If resources were not a hindrance, what would you like to do in the next 6 months? As resources invariably are a hindrance, what plans do you have to achieve your purpose or your dreams and how?

7 As you think about your responses, how would you summarize the top three answers to the question, 'Where are you?' in qualitative terms?

Essential questions for an organization or agency

Again, the answers to questions such as the following are worth writing down, and dating, so that at a later time you can see how much has remained the same, and what has changed.

1 What is your income or turnover? How much of it comes from donations (if any), and if a large percentage, what are the broad sources of those donations (such as standing orders, direct debits, legacies)? Is your income increasing, stable or declining compared with, say, 5 years ago? If increasing, has it kept pace with the rate of inflation? Are you financially independent or resourced to some extent (what percentage?) by a sponsor or parent organization?

2 How many people do you have regular contact with – who get your magazine, buy your products, attend all your events, or come into your shop? How old are they? Are they mainly men or women? If relevant, what is their denomination? Where do they live? How many are outside the UK? How has the total number changed in the past year? How many new attendees do you have and where did they come from? How many have you lost and why?

3 How big is your potential market? If you were highly successful, how many names would you reasonably expect to have on your mailing list, or how many customers might you sensibly expect to have? If you were seriously going to attempt to expand towards your potential, what would you be aiming to do in the next 12 months? Do you realistically have any such plans? If not, why not?

4 How many new products, or innovations, or changes have you introduced in the past, say, 2 years? Where do those new ideas emerge from – the creative thoughts of your central team, the suggestions of your customers, the pressures from the outside world, the deliberations of your trustees or board, or your personal vision? Which of these works best in your situation? Could some of them be more helpful?

5 What do people think of your agency? What percentage of churchgoers would have heard of you? Of Christian leaders? Does your denominational headquarters know you exist? What proportion of your people live in the area where your headquarters are situated? If you are targeting a certain market, such as young people, how many know of you? How would they get to know of you in the first place? In

other words, what is your image among the people you are most seeking to serve?

6 How are you structured? Over the last 2 decades many businesses have deliberately tried to 'flatten out', that is, become less hierarchical. That pattern has not always been followed by UK Christian organizations. One well-known agency I was doing research for had a number of rules which inhibited local initiative, and restricted regional variations. It was seeing decline and one of the reasons was a lack of flexibility in its structure. Could a similar criticism be made of your organization? (The same criticisms can also be made of churches.)

7 As you think about your responses, how would you summarize the top three answers to the question, 'Where are you?', in qualitative terms for your organization?

Where have you come from?

One aspect of the answer to the question, 'Where are you?', is the answer to the question, 'Where were you?'. Adam could have answered, 'in a blissful state looking after the Garden of Eden', but we may not be able to be so positive. To illustrate, your church congregation could be described, both now and where it has come from, in one of three broad ways – declining, stable or growing. The following table, taken from the results of the 2005 English Church Census, shows how the two factors can interrelate.[4]

Table 1.1: Percentages of English churches by how they were changing and how they are now changing

CURRENT POSITION	PAST POSITION	2005
Growing	Growing	5%
Growing	Stable	4%
Growing	Declining	25%
Stable	Growing	4%
Stable	Stable	2%
Stable	Declining	10%
Declining	Growing	12%
Declining	Stable	8%
Declining	Declining	30%

Which of these describes where you are now?

Do not be discouraged!

The purpose of these questions is not to make you feel discouraged or guilty for not having accomplished all that you hoped when first appointed. The first 5 or 10 years rarely go as people optimistically hope. It is easy to look at the declining church numbers and be quite unaware that in the past 10 years half a million people have been added to the church in England across all denominations.[5] That's good news! Likewise, ask yourself how many people have started to come to your church since you became the minister, or how many have been baptized, or come to special events, or your

Christmas services, etc. Or, if working for an agency, how many have come to your meetings, how many donations have you seen, how many legacies, or other positive features of your ministry? It is always easier to look at what you haven't done, than, as the old hymn says, to 'count your blessings, name them one by one, and it will surprise you what the Lord has done'.

You stand on your present accomplishments, large or small, but where do you go next? The aim of answering the question 'Where are you?' is to focus on the future. Alexander the Great may have wept when he had no more worlds to conquer, but the Lord challenges us to keep going forward (Phil. 3:12). Samuel may have 'retired' as judge after he had made Saul king, but he continued his work as intercessor for his people – for almost another 40 years. (1 Sam. 11:15; 12:2,23). We assess the present in order to give due diligence to the future.

The individual context

The question 'Where are you?' can be applied to us as individuals, irrespective of whether we are a Christian leader, minister, or executive with a Christian agency. We may just be an 'ordinary' person in the pew. Stopping from time to time to take stock of our lives is no bad thing. Sometimes the results may surprise us.

Thus, for example, you could write down the answers to such questions as:

1 Give a brief synopsis of your life to this time. Age you left school, any qualifications, any distinctions, any subsequent education, employment history, marital and family status, church life and so on.

2 From this draw out what strengths you see yourself as having, the things you enjoy doing most, the things that other people see you as good at. These three do not necessarily have the same answer. We once had a 15 year old for a week's work experience from school. She always arrived on time, cleared up as she left, and sorted out what we asked her to do very carefully. She was good at computer work, less good with doing calculations. I asked her what she would write on a job application as her skills. 'Computer literacy,' she replied. I agreed but said she should also write, 'A very organized person.' 'Am I?' she replied. She was, but hadn't realized it. What abilities might others notice and mention about you which you might otherwise have missed?

3 You also need to write down your weaknesses both in employment terms and personality terms. Do you have a 'short fuse'? Exaggerate or conceal the truth? Feel jealous? Get frustrated? Do things you prefer others not to know about? Think thoughts that are unhelpful, or worry excessively? It is worth noting down your failures as well as your successes. We all have elements in our character which score plus or minus.

4 If there were no restrictions, what job, or activity would you choose? In other words, what do you wish you were doing right now if you could? Sometimes this question needs to be phrased, 'What do you hope to be doing next year or in five years' time?'. When I was responsible for MARC Europe, we employed a Communications Officer. In her interview I asked, 'Instead of applying for this job, what do you wish you were doing?' She came right back, 'Translating the Bible for a tribe in Africa,' and mentioned the specific

group in which she was interested. She had to earn some money to get the necessary training first, however, which is why she wanted the job.

5 If you are in a long-term job, do your key strengths play into your job description, or would you describe yourself as a square peg in a round hole? It is important to recognize where we are. Our Communications Officer was happy to do her job for two years, but had no intention of staying longer. If we are working in a job when our heart is not really in it, we simply build up enormous frustration within ourselves. I met a minister once who told me frankly, 'I'm only in this job because it's got a good pension,' and not surprisingly there was an enormous dislike and antipathy towards him in his church. It would have been much better all round if he had taken early retirement, but sadly one Christmas his life was terminated by a fatal heart attack.

Why is the last question couched in such negative terms? Simply because there are many in the Christian scene who somehow seem to have lost the thrill for the job they are doing, and often lack either the motivation or the courage to face up to that fact and do something different. On the other hand, there are others who deliberately take on a challenge. In one particular town, an Anglican minister had to be dismissed from his post, but not before almost all his congregation had left. The minister of the parish church, who had exercised a very successful ministry, said to his bishop one day, 'I'm 60 now and have been vicar of this church for 14 years. If you let me become vicar of St John's [the one of the dismissed parson – not the real name] I'll turn it around before I retire.' The bishop agreed, he was duly installed, and while it was hard work, he did succeed, the congregation growing from 20 elderly ladies to having a Christingle Service for 350 people a few years later.

This may be expressed in a different way altogether. In chapter 4 we will talk about vision. Vision is needed for the job we are doing, but we also need to have a personal vision for ourselves. We all have only one life to live, and if Christian, will be asked on the last day how we have multiplied the 'talents' with which we've been entrusted. If we do not know what we would like to achieve personally then we cannot see how that will fit in with the vision we are expected to have for our job. Where the two go hand in hand then you frequently have a successful ministry, but where they are in opposition or simply pulling in different directions, you are likely to fail. Identifying your strengths and weaknesses, and being able to describe what you ultimately wish to do, is not just an academic exercise, but actually a vital necessity if we are to accomplish our goals. As one advert said, 'You've got to plan to become what you plan to become.'

There are numerous books about how to reach your goals from a secular viewpoint;[6] part of the challenge for Christians is how to bring a Christian and biblical mindset to the future-thinking process.

So what comes next?

Whether you have answered these questions for yourself, from a church or organizational viewpoint, you should now know the key factors in your situation. We have suggested identifying the top three, but in some situations there are two crucial factors or perhaps four:

the precise number is far less important than facing up to the key issues. It may seem this is simple and obvious, but many leaders either do not, or cannot, do this. If they are part of a team, very often their team will disagree about their leader's choice of factors. Some leaders have the ability to get to the essential root of a problem. Mike Hill, the Bishop of Bristol, says, 'People seem to think that if we stay as we are, we stay as we are. If we stay as we are, we decline.'[7]

There is a further, more detailed, application which some may find helpful, following Raymond Williams: what are the Residual, Dominant and Emerging elements in your situation?[8] For example, in the church just mentioned which was turned around by a 60-year-old vicar, while the Residual factor was a very small congregation, the Dominant factor was lethargy, which was why it required so much energy to change that church. The Emerging factor was someone who believed it could be changed, or, in other words, had a vision of what the church could become. Other examples could be given. *Back from the Brink* tells the stories of 10 churches about to close which didn't.[9]

Framework

One large Baptist church in Kent assessed where it was, and came to the conclusion that while it was stable, and needed to plan for a new minister as the existing one was due to retire in 2 years' time, its key problem was probably structural – how do you organize your church for growth? In another large Baptist church in Hampshire, the minister said that while he had a similar problem of structure, his biggest difficulty was what to call the leadership – 'elders' was the traditional term used for many decades but it came with overtones (taken from the Scriptures) some of which were simply not relevant in his situation. The minister of a large and growing Independent church in Wales, whose leaders were also called 'elders', also said he was seriously thinking of dropping the term.

These all typify the problem not just of identifying the key factors in your situation but also identifying their priority. Structure, terminology and growth might well have been the issues all three churches would have mentioned, but the priority was different for each church. These factors are all part of the framework within which we have to operate.

Adam presumably was hiding behind some of the abundant vegetation in Eden. He probably couldn't easily move the trees and bushes even if he'd wanted to; they were part of his operating environment. Likewise, our framework is part of our operating environment and it enables us or hinders us. The London Borough of Brent has a large coat of arms on the front of its town hall; it bears the motto 'Forward Together'. Winston Churchill once said, 'If we are together, nothing is impossible. If we are divided, all will fail.' The structure enabling people to work well with each other is thus crucial. God's prime relationship with man is not under his omnipotence but under his covenant[10] – thereby allowing us a freedom but within a broadly secured structure or operating environment.

A mission agency working in Central Asia among Muslim peoples appointed a new International Director a few years ago. He quickly realized that the existing structure inhibited future growth, and proposed an alternative structure which their Executive Committee subsequently approved (and thereby voted themselves out of existence). In the process of explaining the proposed structure, the Director wrote

> Throughout the Scriptures . . . we see how structure is a tool in God's hand. Everything from Creation to Final Judgement has a defined order with predetermined authority, accountability and responsibility. The Trinity itself demonstrates structure in the Godhead.
>
> We have a keen desire to accomplish all that God has for us in the future for his glory. . . . Structure can either enhance the vision God has given us, or hinder it. Through our structure, we can either concentrate authority or diffuse authority. It can enhance our creativity or stifle it. Our structure will either enable us as an effective tool, or place limitations upon us an ineffective tool. Depending on how things are organized, our structure can either frustrate our processes or free them up.[11]

Ensuring that your church or organization has the most appropriate structure to allow growth is crucial. In the UK the 2006 Charities Act has outlined a structure that most churches and agencies will have to follow, though they have been given a few years to implement it. (Publishers have produced various resources to help in this process.[12])

Priorities

There are two key factors in resolving priorities – their urgency and their importance, which might also be expressed as 'their time and their value'.

Some years ago the minister of a church in Southampton wanted to introduce a second morning service as the church was full to overflowing. However, this would mean disrupting the children's work, which ran simultaneously with the main service, as there was only one big hall they could use. When the request was made to the church meeting, the motion was defeated. In the subsequent 12 months, an elder in the church visited every home group to explain the importance of having two services if the church was to grow. When the same motion was put to the church meeting a year later, it was unanimously carried with just one abstention. The minister had decided that it was more important to take the time to carry the church with him, rather than impose two services, however urgent the necessity for growth. In other contexts, urgency is the key factor.

'Importance' can be subdivided into 'minor importance' and 'major importance', and urgency can be sub-divided into 'short-term' and 'long-term'. It may be helpful to locate the issues emerging from your answers to the questions in the following grid.

Table 1.2: The Relationship of Things which are Important and which are Urgent

		IMPORTANCE	
		MINOR	MAJOR
U R G E N C Y	Short-term	Z	Y
	Long-term	Y	X

Issues which end up in the box labelled X will generally be deemed the ones of major priority, followed by those in either of the boxes labelled Y, followed in turn by those in the box labelled Z. Another name for the box labelled X is 'vision', in other words, your key priorities are usually generated by the vision of what you want to achieve, or become.

Types of priorities can also be described in other ways: imagined and real. *Imagined* priorities are the ones we talk about ('our priority is youth work'), describe in our church magazine ('our priority is the prayer meeting') or mention in our church meetings ('our priority is the discipleship of every believer'). *Real* priorities are the ones we actually focus on, that take our time, that influence our decisions and that use our resources most – that is, they reflect our answers to the question 'Where are you?' Real priorities can be categorized as including:

- Putting things right (or teamwork)

- Keeping things going (or daily work)

- Doing new things (or leadership).

Choice

Priorities allow us to identify the key way we are intending to work. Dr Bill Lattimer, a former volunteer with Christian Research, who had been a management structure guru, once defined 'strategy' as 'a small number of big decisions which will affect the future of a church or organization for 3 to 5 years'. It means that someone completes the sentence: 'We are going to do the following . . .'.

The choice of key priorities, however, does not put in place all the detail. Jonathan Nelson is CEO of Providence Equity Partners who made the biggest purchasing deal ever when he bought Bell Canada for $51.5 billion in 2008. Talking to a group of students and parents at Brown University, his Alma Mater, he said, 'You can't at the outset connect the dots. Life does not and should not work that way.'[13]

'Connecting the dots' is not always easy and still requires careful thinking. As an example, suppose you and your spouse were going for a holiday to get some 'relaxation and stimulation'. Which of the following four options would you choose:

a) To go to Margate, because you've always gone to Margate, and you go with your in-laws who look forward to it every year, and who simply love Margate;

b) To fly anywhere in the world for free because you've won a competition;

c) To go to Spring Harvest or New Wine for the teaching and to meet many people;

d) To take the trip of a life-time – to the Base Camp at Everest, even though it will require training, money for equipment and the need to get sponsorship for your charity.

Of course, these four are not mutually exclusive, but the high moral ground of 'always going with your in-laws' might get modified if, say, the second came true. In other words, your choice is bound by a series of factors which all need to be considered before a decision is made and 'the dots' joined up.

Thinking everything through

Where you are may seem a passive description of your current position. In one sense, it is. However, it only remains passive if you stay where you are. It becomes active when you give thought to the direction in which you want to move. Listing the various options (like the holidays) is an initial step. Then come two key questions.

- What do you/your church/your organization want to become in 5 years' time?

- What values will you not sacrifice in order to get there?

We shall consider ways of answering these questions in chapter 4. However, in the answers to the question 'Where are you?' listing some of your values is important. Here are those adopted by Billy Graham early in his ministry.

- 'We will never criticize, condemn or speak negatively about others.'

- 'We will be accountable, particularly in handling finances, with integrity – according to the highest business standards.'

- 'We will tell the truth and be thoroughly honest, especially in reporting statistics.'

- 'We will be exemplary in morals – clear, clean and careful to avoid the very appearance of any impropriety.'[14]

Others put the point negatively. Os Guinness, for example, quotes Kenyan people as saying, 'Westerners have watches but no time. Africans have time but no watches.'[15] Or, again

By our determined efforts to redefine ourselves in ways that are more compelling to the modern world than are faithful to Christ, we have lost not only our identity but our authority and relevance. Our crying need is to be faithful as well as relevant.[16]

Let us earth this in reality. In your church people will join each year, move into your area or transfer to you for whatever reason, while others will leave or move away. Suppose this turnover is 10% in and 10% out each year. In a church of 250 that is 25 new people and 25 leaving, and over the next three years that will be 75 people in and 75 people out. Where are you? A church of 250, but this is not static. What do you want your people to learn and experience in the next three years that would prepare them for ministry in the next church they attend? More importantly, how do you move beyond this static position?

Where are we? We are in a post-modern world and we cannot ignore that contextual factor. A few weeks before he was assassinated, Mahatma Gandhi handed to his grandson, Arun, a talisman upon which were engraved 'Seven Blunders' out of which, said Gandhi, grows the violence that plagues the world. They were a good description of the present world, seen by a man of exceptional vision

Wealth without work
Pleasure without conscience
Knowledge without character
Commerce without morality
Science without humanity
Worship without sacrifice
Politics without principles.[17]

So what does all this say?

The question God asked Adam in the garden, 'Where are you?', needs to be answered carefully as we begin the process of thinking about strategy and vision. It is a here-and-now question, which, while it may be answered passively, implicitly requires movement because none of us can stay as we are, wherever we happen to be. We all have to move on. How we move, and to where we move, depend on many factors, of which the values we wish to espouse are one key element. We will have to choose between different options, and prioritize those which we believe to be the most important or the most urgent.

We need, first of all, to know why we exist (our church or our organization), where we have come from and then to describe in some detail our present position. As we do that some of the factors that are more pressing will almost certainly emerge, elements which might be called 'resources', which are considered in the following chapter. It is, however, only as we know where we are that we can begin to think about where we want to be, or what we want to become, in 5 years' time, and, in order to do that, you may wish to read chapter 6 first before reading the next chapter.

2

WHAT IS THAT IN YOUR HAND?

This is an *encouraging* question, even if Moses must have thought it was a strange one. After all, the answer was obvious – he had a shepherd's crook in his hand (Ex. 4:2). It was probably a well-worn crook too, as Moses would have been a shepherd for well over 30 years by the time God asked him this question, and his staff was doubtless smeared by years of accumulated wool grease, perhaps a few smatterings of blood where sheep had been caught and pulled out of a hole. In effect, like a modern-day bishop, or indeed shepherd, his staff was, as it were, his badge of office. Any stranger meeting Moses in the desert would instantly know his occupation.

Moses would have known that crook very well – where the knots in the wood were, the best position to lever something out, the strongest place to hold it to knock something down – in the same way that we know the gifts of the people who work with us, their strengths and weaknesses. We have learned the ways of the institution, so no surprises there. We are in charge of our world, and mostly we reckon we've got it sussed. Like Moses, we never think the Holy Spirit might have something to show us outside of what we already know and understand. Nothing changes here, I know my way around.

So Moses simply said, 'A staff,' just as we might have said, '120 on an average Sunday,' or 'There's the youth worker and a part-time secretary,' or 'Our average turnover is £250,000.'

'Throw it on the ground,' says God, and Moses, obediently (his usual way) does so. 'Why don't you start an extra service?' or 'Should you not hold a seminar on this?' and we, obediently, make the necessary arrangements.

That was when Moses got the fright of his life – well, perhaps the second greatest fright. Hearing the Lord speak out of the burning bush was almost certainly one of the biggest frights anyone could have. The staff had become a snake. Moses knew the snake hadn't just appeared, and, in any case, his staff was now nowhere to be seen. It had become a real snake squirming around all over the place. It was as if an extra 60 people had come to your church last Sunday – why did they? And someone had put a £1,000 cheque in the collection! And your part-time secretary volunteered to work full-time, the extra days totally gratis. 'I thought your husband was against you doing that,' you'd said. 'Jim's changed his mind; sees the importance of what the organization is doing,' she replied.

The ordinary simply becomes the extraordinary. What would never occur to you in a thousand years has just happened – the evidence is in front of you. A minister felt he should pray for someone's leg to be healed, so he did. Fred limped out of the door at the end of the service as usual. 'I was praying for you,' the minister said. 'I know,' said Fred, and carried on limping away. Ten seconds later he was back shouting, 'Vicar, my leg's healed, it happened this second!' (This is a true story from an Anglican minister in Kent.)

Your world will never be quite the same ever again. The miracle has taken place.

'Pick it up,' says God, so Moses, obediently, gets hold of the snake's tail – and instantly it's his old shepherd's staff, which he knows so well, back again in his hand. Familiarity restored. I suspect, however, that Moses took a great deal more care of that staff after that – after all, he never knew when it might turn into a snake again (especially when, after confronting Pharaoh, he finds it is a snake-eating snake/staff as well).

'What is that in your hand?' In Moses' case, resources he had never thought twice about before. What resources do you have at hand? It's worth just thinking about what God has already given to you. Some of your resources will already have been pinpointed by the replies to the questions in chapter 1 – where are you? You have that many people attending on a Sunday, a staff of such-and-such size, an income of so-and-so, a magazine with this circulation, an agency with this size income, a loving family with this many children, a salary of such-and-such, a car or other vehicle, this sort of computer, and so on. These are the basic resources by which you live. There are others, like, perhaps, reasonably good health, a fair amount of energy, a clear commitment to follow Christ or the privilege of being appointed to your present position, which could be added to the list.

But the question 'What is that in our hand?' really goes deeper than a simple list of items, and the following categories suggest other ways in which the question can be answered.

Physical resources

Your 'plant' is a key resource, including the building where you worship and your church hall, or your headquarters building, with perhaps outbuildings of various kinds. It can also include less obvious items: in the early days of colour photocopying, one church in Kent bought a colour photocopier which enabled them to produce a full-colour magazine. They didn't use it all the time, and were willing to allow others to pay to use it as well, rather than go to a local shop.

Another church, an Anglican church, had bought a pair of extremely high stepladders to enable them to put in new light bulbs 40 or 50 feet above the congregation when necessary. Likewise they were happy to lend these to someone else (although the problem of transporting them was left to the borrower).

More tangible physical resources might include a T-Loop for the hard-of-hearing, a data projector for use during the services, or a good sound system. Organizations may have a linked computer system or other specialized equipment to enable them to do their work. Again, before reading on, stop for a moment, and note the physical resources you have at hand:

Physical resources_____

_____

Human resources

Resources are not purely financial or physical, of course. You need to consider those who are helping you, who may be members of your family, your immediate leadership team, people on your PCC or elders or other committees, the volunteers who contribute in so many ways, and other 'HR', human resources. These can be measured in terms of numbers, but sometimes it is worth listing them in terms of skills or attributes, or degree of commitment.

A Pentecostal minister who came to a MARC Europe seminar once was quite worried – he wanted to extend his church as it was too small for the current congregation. He had plenty of ideas about what should be done but didn't have a qualified architect in his congregation, nor did he know where to find one he could trust. In that seminar we did an exercise thinking through possibilities, and the minister suddenly shouted out to everyone, 'I've got it!' He had thought of where he could find an architect – the local pub had recently opened an excellently designed extension – he would ask the architect who had done that. He went away from the seminar satisfied.

That minister was looking for a particular gift to help him in the way forward. Knowing what gifting you are going to require for the future is a crucial part of HR. When appointing new trustees some charities compile a kind of 'gift register' – what the existing trustees bring to their job. By appraising the existing gifts, gaps can be identified and filled.

What are the human resources you have at hand?

Human resources_____

_____

Strategic thinking

The ability to think ahead is crucial, and is looked at in more detail in chapter 4. It is, however, worth pausing to reflect from where, or on whom, you get your key forward planning and understanding.

David Bowden, the CEO of one of the largest research companies in the world, TNS, said, 'There will be an ongoing move towards providing insight to clients who are looking harder for a return on their investment.'[18] However, insight is not always easily come by. As Henry Ford apparently stated, 'If I'd asked the public, they would have said they wanted a faster horse.'[19] The ability to think strategically and to live strategically is not easy, but in the parable of the shrewd manager, Jesus said in Luke 16:8, 'The master commended the dishonest manager because he had acted shrewdly' (not because he was dishonest). David Beer, CEO of Purpose Driven Europe, argued that leadership must have access to strategic thinking if it is to be successful.[20] The historian Arnold Toynbee wrote 'someone trying to understand the present is like a man with his nose pressed against a mirror trying to see his whole body.'[21] Hence insight is not a luxury, but an essential. Where do you get your strategy from?

We get our strategic thinking from_____

_____

Financial resources

If you look after a church, have you ever worked out what the average income of your congregation might be? How much per week (or per month or year if that is easier) would those in your congregation who come from the local estate take home? How much those who live in the middle-class estate at the top of the hill? What about the pensioners: how many of them are living on just the state pension and how many have a private pension or income? Add it all up. If that is the total congregational income, how much is given to the church? This is not just an academic exercise. A number of black churches do precisely this kind of calculation, and use the results to suggest how much more should be tithed to the church! For example, when they have added up how much has been given in the collection, if it's not enough, they send the bags round again! From these figures can you work out if most in your congregation tithe? Are you always having to ask for money or is the situation such that you dare not mention it, let alone preach about it?

Is the income to your church, or organization, increasing in line with inflation, or below it? How has it changed in past years? (While present and future inflation cannot be given, past inflation rates have been published if you wish to look at the trend over the past few years.[22]) Just pause for a moment, and write down some of the key financial resources you have at hand:

Financial resources_____

_____

Relationships

One aspect of the human resources consideration is the relationships present. These depend on the people you have, but are an extension of your opportunities. St Thomas' Church in Lancaster is situated right next to the police station; that allowed the minister, Canon Peter Guinness, to meet with the local Chief Constable from time to time – an important relationship not available to everyone.

I once attended a service in a Milton Keynes church at which the local Lord Lieutenant was present. Not meeting such people very often, I went up to him and asked him what Lord Lieutenants do, and was fascinated by the range of duties he undertook. A church which has such a person in its congregation, at least occasionally, has an important relationship which can perhaps be used for the good of the kingdom.

A church will have its list of members, and an organization will usually have a mailing list or list of customers or donors. It is worth recording on such lists (there are many computer programmes enabling this to be done easily) whatever positive characteristics one may know of such people, though this should be kept confidential. One minister, now retired, kept a list which included not just the age of each person, their family details and occupation, but also a brief summary of every significant conversation which the minister had had with that person, purely for his own private use. (It may well be that this practice now infringes on basic data protection policies.) Obviously, that made it highly confidential and personal, but the minister used this list to pray for these different people for the first hour of every working day. As a consequence he had an uncanny ability to remember the different circumstances of the folk in his church, and his pastoral work was immensely strengthened by such a system.

A different sort of relationship will be built up with people who come to church activities during the week but do not attend on Sunday. These kinds of groups, sometimes called 'the fringe', are extremely vital for enabling the church to grow. Having a list, for example, of all the mothers (and fathers) who use the parents and toddlers group enables a church to hold a special Alpha course for them (at a time they can come, perhaps during the day). After-school clubs, luncheon clubs, coffee mornings, counselling services, practical help such as gardening for older people – all provide some kind of relationship which can be used, as opportunity allows, for witness and other involvement.

The same is true of non-church or para-church organizations. There are those who regularly support or use your services – your inner core, as it were. There will be others who give occasionally, pray for your work, or are interested enough to take your newsletter, as well as others who have heard of you even if they have never given you their name and address. All these reflect different kinds of relationships, and give different kinds of opportunities to explore.

My wife and I are trustees of Kisumu Children, an organization helping needy children in Kisumu (the third largest city in Kenya), through an orphanage and in other ways. One of the opportunities which has emerged from that work has been the formation of the Kisumu Children's Leaders' Forum, a twice-a-year gathering for those working with children in any way in Kisumu – other children's homes, the clergy, the police, the local remand centre, the children's department, the social care department, and so on. They meet to share together what each of them is doing, and to have some management or leadership training. This results in a huge interacting bundle of relationships, but with a common theme (working with children) and an opportunity to work and think together.

Then there are the whole set of relationships outside your immediate circle – other clergy in your area, Churches Together perhaps, local schools, other agencies and organizations whose work is similar to yours or has an affinity to it.

What are the key relationships you have at hand?

Relationships_____

_____

Image

One of the things at hand, like it or not, is your image. What do people think about you? If you were walking down the road and met a friend and you started talking about a mutual third acquaintance, you might say, 'Oh, yes, Jonathan, he's a good guy, he works with absolute integrity, and is always checking the facts he has are correct.' Then, in effect, you are describing Jonathan's image as you have seen it – in this case, an upright, true man. But supposing two friends were talking about you – what sort of words would they use to describe you? Would they be positive, positive with 'buts', negatives with 'but you must remember that' or purely negative?

The same kind of image relates to churches and organizations. Someone once said of their local church, 'St John's? Yes, that's the church which does very good funerals!' It might not have been the image you would have chosen but at least it's positive. Having a good image is worth its weight in gold. It may take years to build a reputation for accuracy, always completing a job when asked to do something, being comprehensive not narrow, but such reputations (or images) can be lost overnight by a thoughtless mistake with high-profile consequences. The work of decades can literally be dashed in seconds.

In the 1980s, a well-known pastor of a large American church, in a moment of temptation in a pastoral situation, committed adultery, and resigned his pastorate. He publicly repented of his actions, and the Lord in his goodness enabled him to recover his position, and 10 or so years later he again became the pastor of a large church. While his ministry continues as a blessing to many, his image is always tarnished by what happened, because we sadly ignore the plank in our own eye and focus on the specks in our brother's eye.

Our image derives in part from our history. Knowing where we have come from may give us clues as to where we are now, but image is derived less from basic knowledge of the past than from the values utilized in the past. What are or were the things that drove the church, your agency, or you yourself in days gone by?

Images, like rituals, are not static. Olive Drane argues that 'it is now a commonplace sight to come across flowers and other icons fastened to fences by the roadside, marking the spot where someone has died.'[23] These should not be dismissed as mere sentimentality. A physical presence can create an image, and so can a new letterhead, a more colourful logo, a renewed website. A changed physical image can generate excitement, a sense of newness, as if saying 'Come . . . explore with me.'

What is your image? What is it that you have at hand in this respect? Write it down, for yourself and, if appropriate, for your church or agency:

Your personal image_____

_____

_____

Your church or organization's image_____

_____

_____

Identity

Similar in some ways to your image is your identity. This is who you are, a unique individual, fashioned by God, and the only one quite like you in 6.7 billion people in the world. What are the key things about you which are important? I went to the nurse the other day to get another yellow fever injection: her key question was 'Are you in reasonable health for a person of your age?' – two elements of my identity were required, my fitness and year of birth. What are the elements about you that are important for the work you are doing? Your name? Your gender? Your previous experience? Your academic qualifications? Your family history? Your marital status? Your character (which tends to merge with your image)? Your ability to drive a car, or a bus? Your energy?

If you are a church or an organization, similar questions can be asked, of which your name is probably one of the most important. Image and identity work here very closely. I was once in Athens when a lady pushed by me. 'Oh, thank goodness,' she was saying, 'there's a McDonald's – they'll have clean toilets!' In a totally different context, I sometimes help facilitate events for larger churches. Here, size of the regular congregation is the key identity factor, not even denomination. At other times, location will be important. 'I want to work in the north of England,' one of our children said, and wouldn't even look at suitable vacancies in the south.

Pause for a moment, and write down three or four key elements fashioning your identity.

Your identity_____

_____

_____

Structure

One resource which is often more important for churches and organizations than individuals is your operational structure, or the basis on which you work. There are a number of churches, for example, which find it very difficult to grow because their structure isn't correct. There are some ministers, for instance, who are very controlling, and want to ensure that everything that happens in the church happens through them. That simply stultifies growth. You cannot chair the missions committee, the evangelism committee, the discipleship committee, the pastoral committee and the youth committee all equally efficiently, unless your church is tiny. In those circumstances, the minister simply becomes a bottleneck, inhibiting progress. People get tired of such centralization, and begin to leave out of frustration at lack of movement.

However, the same can happen at the next level up, and is perhaps seen more in Baptist and Independent churches than others as these operate very much on a congregational model. Asking the members to approve every major decision can also inhibit action and, ultimately, growth. One Baptist church grew sufficiently large that the congregation was asked to agree that the elders could make most of the decisions about the worship and programme without consulting them first. There was plenty of discussion, but it was agreed, freeing up the decision-making process and allowing the church to expand further (which it did).

The 2006 Charities Act has similarly caused many churches and organizations to consider the differences between legal responsibilities (handled by trustees), spiritual responsibilities (handled by elders or PCC members) and practical responsibilities (handled by deacons or some PCC members). A structure which clearly delineates these differing responsibilities allows the decision-making processes to work more smoothly, and thus potentially enables the church or organization to be more efficient, and thus more effective.

A Dell advertisement had the strapline 'Your competitive edge is becoming dull' because of the complexity caused by some companies' IT systems. Dell, of course, offered to reduce it. The point, however, is well-made – whether your systems are governed electronically or non-electronically it is perfectly possible for your structure to inhibit growth.[24]

If you are in a church or agency, pause for a moment and consider whether the decision-making structure is the most suitable for your work and its potential future. If it isn't, in what ways do you think it could be changed?

I think our structure_____

_____

_____

Commitment

A critical element of what you may have at hand is your personal commitment to the task in which you are engaged, or the collective commitment of your staff team, your leadership, or your members to what you are wanting to do. How can you assess commitment? Look at people's readiness to do things that are not immediately noticed, to volunteer to do a further task, to work the extra hour, or to help someone in their job.

In one church, the minister was asked to visit an old man. He found that he and his wife were in poor health but wanted to sit out in their garden when the weather was suitable. However the path from the back door to the patio was broken up and needed replacing. He offered to do it himself, and next Sunday at church asked if anyone would be free to help him the following Thursday. Several turned up – that was commitment, a willingness to help in the name of Christ. Hope 2008 was a major programme initiated by Youth for Christ, Soul Survivor, the Message Trust and others which rapidly spread across the country and caused hundreds of volunteers to engage in 'good works' for their local community. Whatever the results that emerged from such actions, the commitment of thousands of young people and older people was impressive.

What mark out of 10 would you give the collective commitment in your church or organization? If you are thinking of answering as an individual, what score out of 10 would you rate your commitment to your faith, your wife or husband, your family, your work, your church and your hobbies? Someone once said, 'Excellence is not being the best; it is doing your best.'[25] It is important to recognize that in the teams of which we are a part.

I think the top three collective commitments in our church/organization are:

1)_____

2)_____

3)_____

Motivation

Commitment and motivation are similar in some ways, but while commitment looks at what you might do motivation describes why you are doing it. It is therefore sometimes more difficult to define as it relates to vision. As an individual you may not know what you want to accomplish in your life by the time you are, say, 60 – you may not think of becoming a headteacher, or earning a salary of £50,000, although some do set themselves such goals and work towards them.

John Goddard has a most dramatic record of personal purposes and goals. When he was 15 years old he heard his grandmother saying, 'If only I'd done this when I was young,' and resolved he never wanted to say that when he was a grandfather. So he made a list of what he wanted to do: 10 rivers to explore; 17 mountains to climb; have a career in medicine; visit every country in the world; learn to fly a plane; retrace the travels of Marco Polo; ride a horse in the Pasadena Rose Parade; read the entire Bible, Encyclopaedia Britannica, and the works of Shakespeare, Plato, Aristotle, Dickens and a dozen other authors; become an Eagle Scout; dive in a submarine; play the flute and violin; go on a church mission; marry; and have children (he had five). He had a list of 127 goals, and by the time he was 47 (in 1972) he had accomplished 103 of them. As a result, he became a highly paid lecturer and toured the world telling his adventures.[26]

Most of us are not like John Goddard. That doesn't stop us having a basic motivation for our life – 'to serve the Lord', 'to count for God', 'to follow Christ wherever he leads' – some such phrase will be true for many Christians. Perhaps, however, you've never stopped to sum up in such a statement what your motivation or motivations might be. Is it to *accomplish something* or to *become something*? There is a great difference. To *give* or to *get*? In many ways these are the two key motivations: which of them is yours? As Winston Churchill said, 'We make a living by what we get, we make a life by what we give.'[27]

I know a well-to-do man who was converted in his forties, but found it very hard to lay down the basic motivation of accumulating money (at which he was expert) after becoming a Christian. Some research has shown the attitudes to life that we have at 20 are essentially those that guide us for life – unless, of course, like Moses, God suddenly asks us, 'What is that in your hand?' and we find a whole new wealth of spiritual energy of which we had hitherto been unaware.

In the 1930s a Johns Hopkins professor asked his students to choose 200 boys aged 12 to 16 living in the nearby slums, investigate their background and environment and then predict their future. The students completed the exercise and concluded that 90% would spend some time in jail. The professor gave another group of students 25 years later the task of testing that prediction. They managed to get in touch with 180 of the original 200 and found only 4 had been in jail. Why was it that these men, coming from such a poor background, had had such a surprisingly good record? The researchers were continually told, 'Well, there was a teacher . . .' They found that in 75% of cases it was the same woman, now living in a retired teachers' home. Could she give any reason why these boys should have remembered her? 'No,' she said, 'no, I really couldn't.' And then, thinking back over the years, she said musingly, more to herself than her questioners: '*I loved those boys* . . .'.[28] Your motivation can have a huge impact on others!

The most significant factor in your personal history is you. In western societies, outside emergencies like wars, you are fundamentally the reason for all the outcomes you are experiencing. So what is it that motivates you?

- Is it the *abilities* you have (for learning, researching, leading, organizing, evaluating, influencing, communicating)?

- Is it the *subject matter* you work with (the knowledge, the information, the particulars, the characteristics)?

- Is it the *circumstances* you work or live within (the visibility, the newness, the difference, the structure, the building, the orderliness)?

- Is it the *operating relationship* you work for (being part of the team, your boss, being a leader of others)?

- Is it the likely *pay-off* (the perks, the salary, the influence, the recognition, the information, the ability to fulfil your ambition)?[29]

What are your motivations? This is a personal question. It's not how large your church or organization might be in 5 years' time, but simply what is it that guides your life? Write it down, and make it brief enough to fit on just one line:

_____

What is that in your hand?

The above comments may perhaps be summarized in three broad areas of resources: your relationships, your image and your opportunities.

On an individual level, what is at hand reflects the work experience you have, your personality, what your friends like (and dislike) about you, and the spiritual motivations of your vision. Ultimately, what is it in your heart that God can use?

On a church or organizational level, what is at hand includes what people think of your church or agency, the resources you possess and can work with, the values you espouse, your internal relationships and ways of working, your collective commitment. Ultimately, what is your vision, and how worthwhile is it?

However, such questions can be difficult or even impossible to answer personally. One reason is that some people may know others fairly well, but they don't know themselves. A principal of a theological college once told me that his students seemed unaware of who they were, or what type of person they were.

For a number of years Christian Research ran a 2-day conference that we all called 'Kick-it', actually spelled KYKYT and standing for Know Yourself Know Your Team. It was quite popular, with the first day of the two going through a number of exercises to help people better understand their personality, their administrative ability, the way they communicated with others (did they talk as adults, teachers or children?), what they contributed as a member of a team, or their basic motivations (were they an affiliator, an achiever or an influencer, or all three?). Many books have been written on such topics, including an excellent one on motivation by David Cormack.[30]

How people contributed as a team member was one of the five aspects of self-knowledge which seemed especially helpful – so as a practical exercise it is included here.

Belbin's work on teams

Meredith Belbin was a management consultant at the Henley College of Management for a number of years in the 1970s and also undertook a similar role in Australia. It was in these locations that he made his far-reaching observations on the nature of management teams. His key observation was that those working in team situations bring one or more of eight key skills to that task, though very few bring six or more.

However, he recognized that not all the various combinations of these characteristics actually produce successful teams. There are some combinations which simply don't work. His book *Management Teams* (see bibliography) explains his ideas – it is so popular it has been reprinted virtually every year since first published. In his more recent writings he has introduced a ninth type, the specialist who functions as a team member on a part-time basis usually only while their particular topic is being discussed – such as an architect brought in to a planning meeting which is looking at building an extension to a church.

Meredith Belbin produced a self-perception inventory which helped people to identify which of these different characteristics they have. It has been found to be remarkably robust, and consistent over time, across ages, for both genders, and in different cultures and ethnic groups. A considerably adapted version of this was produced for use in MARC Europe seminars, and by answering these questions the different characteristics can be ascertained for a particular individual.

Teamwork questionnaire

Answer the following questions about yourself on the basis that if the statement is generally true of you, you score 2, if it is sometimes true of you, you score 1, and if it not true of you, you score 0.

1	I am a creative thinker	
2	I am a stickler for accuracy	
3	I have a flair for ordering people and situations	
4	I like to be aware of the broader picture	
5	I usually hit the nail on the head	
6	I feel I make significant contribution in group thinking	
7	I hate not to complete a task	
8	I am not thrown by having to cooperate with those who are not like minded	
9	My creativity may be stifled by being part of a team	
10	I have most rapport with those who have a positive contribution to make	

11	I find my broad circle of relationships essential	
12	I am not influenced in decisions by my personal feelings	___
13	I enjoy having a persuasive role among my working colleagues	___
14	I focus on achieving goals	___
15	I feel it is vital to give equal consideration to minor issues as well as major	___
16	I feel I can contribute positively to the difficulties of colleagues	___
17	I am able to discern the pros and cons of various suggestions	___
18	I can frequently shed fresh light on intractable difficulties	___
19	I have the ability to knit together different ideas	___
20	I never leave a task unfinished	___
21	I relish investigating fresh horizons	___
22	I respond well to plainly set out targets	___
23	I feel it important to have a good understanding of my colleagues	___
24	I am not concerned with being liked in presenting my ideas	___
25	Difficulties stimulate my originality	___
26	My approach is down-to earth rather than theoretical	___
27	I put in considerable effort to maintain harmony among my colleagues	___
28	I can distinguish unworkable options	___
29	I am aware of the avenues to be followed if specialist knowledge is required	___
30	I would rather be a supporter than an instigator	___
31	I enjoy tasks which need intense focus	___
32	I am prepared to stress my own opinions at all times	___
33	I have amicable relationships with my colleagues and put considerable effort into such	___
34	I am able to take an unbiased position with regard to difficulties	___
35	I work at a consistent rate however stressful life may be	___

36	I am a dominant personality but am not unaware of the situations of other people	____
37	When required, I have no hesitation in assuming a position of authority	____
38	I feel it is important to be up-to-date with new approaches and progress	____
39	I am not in a hurry to come to ill-considered conclusions	____
40	I am completely happy when being stretched	____
41	As events develop, I can apply suggestions successfully	____
42	I hate misuse of opportunity	____
43	I am strong at bringing together opposing situations and views	____
44	I am happy to move with the flow when it is sound	____
45	I am motivated by time considerations in completing tasks	____
46	I pursue suggestions and personnel which seem significant	____
47	I like to analyze difficulties rather than opting for quick-fire solutions	____
48	I appreciate a logical progression in tasks based or an overall strategy	____
49	I have no difficulty in marketing a programme of which I approve	____
50	My approach is imaginative as well as logical	____
51	I have no hesitation in expressing myself, forcibly if necessary	____
52	On most occasions, I can weigh up a situation impartially	____
53	It is important to me to have clearly delineated boundaries for my projects	____
54	I like to be unbiased in my approach, able to see all sides of a situation	____
55	I am concerned with the needs of others	____
56	I am always alert for problems	____

Now enter your scores for each answer into the grid below and then add up the total you have for each of the letters A, B, C . . . G, H.

No	A	B	C	D	E	F	G	H	No	A	B	C	D	E	F	G	H
1	☐								29				☐				
2			☐						30						☐		
3						☐			31			☐					
4				☐					32								☐
5		☐							33						☐		
6								☐	34	☐							
7					☐				35					☐			
8						☐			36							☐	
9	☐								37								☐
10						☐			38				☐				
11				☐					39		☐						
12		☐							40			☐					
13								☐	41	☐							
14					☐				42				☐				
15			☐						43							☐	
16						☐			44						☐		
17		☐							45			☐					
18	☐								46				☐				
19							☐		47		☐						
20			☐						48					☐			
21				☐					49				☐				
22					☐				50	☐							
23						☐			51								☐
24								☐	52							☐	
25	☐								53					☐			
26					☐				54		☐						
27							☐		55						☐		
28			☐						56			☐					

Grand Total

In this way you should have scores between 0 and 14 points for each letter. A person with 14 for a particular attribute is not necessarily twice as good as somebody with a score of 7 for the same attribute, since we all score ourselves with differing degrees of strength. It is therefore not so much the magnitude of the score which you may have obtained but the ones which are highest.

It is also important to look at the differences between your scores and observe where the differences are greatest. The attributes whose scores are higher than the largest difference will be the ones that describe you best. Suppose you scored a 14, 13, 12 and 10 for four attributes. The first three differ by only one point but there is a difference of two points between the third and the fourth. It is likely that the first three really represent your particular attributes, and the fourth could be discounted. It is possible to get a detailed sophisticated analysis that delves into your answers more deeply, but in this particular exercise we suggest you simply focus on your two or three highest scores (in a few cases four or even five scores).

One of the disadvantages of Belbin's work is that he uses what seem to be strange names for some of his attributes (the reason for which is explained in *Management Teams*). The terms used below are understandable descriptions of each attribute. The key thing is to look at the two or three attributes, maybe more, maybe fewer, in which you are strongest and to note the strengths and weaknesses of these.

The eight attributes which Belbin focuses on may be divided into four pairs, each along a given axis.

The Thinking Axis:

- *A* are those with a *creative* mind, constantly able to think of new ideas, not only in terms of products but also in terms of relationships. Creative people may not necessarily be good 'people-people' but they are often good at thinking how difficult relationships can be resolved.

- *B* are *critical* people who in many ways are the reverse of the creative and frequently can tell creative people why their ideas will not work. This leads to a natural tension between them but that tension is not usually destructive.

The Information Axis:

- *C* represents the *detailed* people who are excellent at proof-reading, making sure minute things are correct, and will invariably ensure that the total on a page of numbers tallies.

- *D* are the *resource* people who frequently know where to find something, know where to go to get a certain skill, or know people who do. They are excellent at networking and highly useful in situations where many different types of need may be present. Many clergy are resource people.

The Work Axis is divided between:

- Those who are *E task* people, who like to get jobs completed, and

- *F relational* people whose joy is to meet people and share with them.

Both are needed in work situations, and help make any church or organization run more smoothly.

The Leadership Axis comprises:
- G the *director* or co-ordinator type, usually with good inter-personal skills, and

- H the *shaper*, a driver who often makes things happen by using the force of their personality or the present circumstances.

The Shaper operates on the principle 'Why?' – what is the reason for this particular action, what is its purpose, what do we hope to achieve by doing this? The Director operates on the basis of 'How?' and seeks to indicate the ways by which actions can be fulfilled, how a vision can be worked out, the mechanisms that need to be in place in order to ensure that something happens. Often, but not always, the Director is better with people than a Shaper. It is these two on a team together who can bring intolerable strain on relationships because of their different approaches to leadership, and some teams break under that strain.

In a team of a small number of people, say six or less, those present will need to exercise two or more of their particular strengths. Those who are part of a larger team, say sixteen people or more, may well find that there are two or three others present who have a dominant strength similar to theirs.

If you have two scores on any particular axis which are very close or even identical (which is quite common) it simply means you have the advantage of being able to understand both points of view, but people will often not know which viewpoint you are representing at any particular moment. It therefore helps if you give some indication of which side you are coming from. If, for example, you are equally a creative person and a critic, you might wish to preface some of your comments by

God's Questions

saying something like 'That's a good idea, why don't we . . .' or 'I am not sure I agree with that because . . .'. Such phrases subconsciously indicate to everyone else which particular attribute you are about to use.

If doing the exercise for a whole team it may be interesting to discuss which category each of the 12 apostles fits into. Some will fit more than one.[31]

The following table summarizes the features of each type and the qualities and weaknesses associated with each. Chapter 7 describes these various characteristics in much more detail.

Table 2.1: Features of the different characteristics described by Belbin

TYPE	TYPICAL FEATURES	POSITIVE QUALITIES	ALLOWABLE WEAKNESSES

A Creative	Individualistic
	Serious minded
	Unorthodox
		Imagination
		Intellect
		Knowledge
			Up in the clouds
			Inclined to disregard
			  the practical details
			  or protocol

B Critical	Sober Unemotional Prudent	Judgement Discretion Hard-headedness	Lacks inspiration Lacks ability to motivate others

C Detailed	Painstakingly orderly
	Conscientious
	Anxious
		A capacity for
		  follow through
		Perfectionism
			Reluctance to 'let go'
			Tendency to worry
			  about small things

D Resourcer	Extrovert
	Enthusiastic
	Curious
	Communicative
		Capacity for
		  contacting people
		  and exploring
		  anything new
		Ability to respond
		  to challenge
			Liable to lose interest
			  once the initial
			  fascination has
			  passed

E Task	Conservative
	Dutiful
	Predictable
		Organizing ability
		Practical common
		  sense
		Hardworking
		Self-discipline
			Lack of flexibility
			Unresponsive to
			  unproven ideas

TYPE	TYPICAL FEATURES	POSITIVE QUALITIES	ALLOWABLE WEAKNESSES
F Team	Socially orientated Rather mild Sensitive	Ability to respond to people and to situations Promotes team spirit	Indecisive in moments of crisis
G Director	Calm Self-confident Controlled	Capacity for treating and welcoming all potential contributors on their merits and without prejudice Strong sense of objectives	Not necessarily especially strong in terms of intellect or creative ability
H Shaper	Highly strung Outgoing Dynamic	Drive and readiness to challenge inertia, ineffectiveness, complacency or self deception	Prone to provocation, irritation and impatience

Which are your characteristics by the above analysis? Do you agree with how you are described? Such knowledge is also now part of what you have at hand. Richard Bryan of the QA Research Company says, 'Don't overestimate your own knowledge. Always know who to ask for advice. Understanding what you can and can't do is a key part of being a leader.'[32]

3

WHAT ARE YOU DOING HERE?

This is a *challenging* question. The prophet Elijah had courageously taken a stand for the living God facing up to 850 priests of Baal in calling down fire from heaven to consume the sacrifice which was being offered. Elijah's God had answered and Baal's priests were now dead. Queen Jezebel threatened the same fate for Elijah, so he ran for his life, some 250 miles from Mount Carmel to Mount Horeb ('the mount of God') on the Sinai Peninsula. Although supernaturally fed for his flight, after 40 days on the move he was doubtless exhausted. He sat down under a tree on the slopes of Mount Sinai (which the Israelites had taken 40 years to reach over 500 years before) and prayed he might die.

An angel speaks to him and then comes a question from the Lord. Elijah was used to hearing God speak to him, so he knew who it was. 'What are you doing here?' Elijah probably thought there was a fairly obvious answer, especially as God had sent an angel twice to give him some food to get there. However, he didn't reply, 'Just getting over that marathon journey' or 'Running away from Jezebel'. He gave a more serious, evaluative reflection: 'I've been very zealous for you, Lord, in a nation which has deserted you, and now they're after me also' (my paraphrase of 1 Kgs 19:10). Elijah was unaware of anyone else faithful to God, and God had to tell him he'd overlooked a few thousand others – he wasn't ready to see the width of God's work.[33]

Elijah was told to go and stand on the mountain. He did so. There was an ear-splitting noise as the wind howled around him and the rocks crashed down and parts of the mountain split before him. He didn't, and couldn't, ignore that! Many observers would have been terrified and at the end of their wits. The storm smashed into Elijah's senses, and however tired he felt, this would have forced him into high alert. Some tornadoes today have that kind of power and wreak havoc and devastation on everything in their path. A few people, self-titled 'storm-chasers', deliberately seek them out to take dramatic photos, but most ordinary folk take shelter or flee as fast as possible.[34]

Then came an earthquake. I was once part of a group visiting Egypt, staying in a hotel in Cairo. At about 6.30 a.m. one morning I had made myself a cup of tea and was sitting on my bed reading my Bible. To my surprise, the tea in the cup suddenly took on a life of its own and sloshed over the edge. I wondered what on earth was happening, and then hearing a glass in the bathroom fall off its shelf, realized it was an earthquake. I did what I now know was foolish, and ran to the window (you should stand in a doorframe so that if the building collapses, the frame may protect you), and then went to the bedroom door. Several others had woken up and had also come to their doors. Deciding it was now all over (it only lasted a few seconds) and that as the hotel hadn't collapsed we were safe, we returned to our rooms! We found out later that it had been a force 6.1 earthquake on the Richter scale and the epicentre was 15 miles away.

It was what I would call a 'Now' moment. I didn't stop to finish my tea, nor read to the end of the chapter. The immediate need took precedence over anything and everything else I happened to be doing. Something had intruded to demand instant attention. Perhaps God sent Elijah an earthquake to jerk him into a 'Now' moment, where the present circumstances take precedence over the past. 'Elijah, I didn't ask you what you have been doing the past 20 years, but *what are you doing here?*' Perhaps also, in view of his circumstances and the fact he was bordering on despair, he needed a fresh demonstration of God's absolute and awe-inspiring power.

The earthquake was followed by a fire. We can all visualize the panic which can ensue in the urgency to get out of a burning building. I have never been in a serious fire, and have no wish to be, but imagine that the same kind of riveting presence of the 'Now' is again forced upon one. You don't bother to finish your drink when every second counts to escape. Your one concern is to get away.

The storm, of course, was also a 'Now' moment. This was not the kind of gale in which you watch the rain lashing down in the garden through the windows of your lounge, but rather one in which you would run for safety. So, three times God effectively said to Elijah, 'Wake up! Wake up! Wake up! I am asking you a present-tense question. *What are you doing here?*'

It's a question most of us dislike. What are you doing right now in your ministry? In your church? In your home? In your organization? No, the question is not, how many people came on average last year, nor how many meetings you held last week, nor how many visitors you had this past month, nor how much money was given last quarter, nor how well your team is functioning, nor what you are hoping to do next year? It is the awkward, present-tense question 'What are you doing, right now?' What are your attitudes? Your actions today? Your real feelings about the people you work with? Your motives for making that phone call, or writing that letter or email? What do you really think about that project to which you have given only half-hearted support? King Saul had a promising start as the first king of Israel, but he didn't follow what Samuel told him, disobeying God's instructions to kill off all the Amalekites, and finally he used a medium to seek to speak to the dead Samuel. He wasn't the real thing, but hiding behind his position. Could you be hiding behind your position? Are you the real thing?

'What are you doing here?' God asked Elijah a second time. But Elijah had failed to recognize the significance of his experience with storm, quake and fire and gave the Lord the same answer as before – what he *had* been doing. In modern-day thinking, it would seem that the Lord then implemented his purpose to retire Elijah, as he had fulfilled his calling. He was told to go and appoint his successor, anoint a couple of people who would be important in God's purposes (even if they wreaked havoc on his people Israel). Once he'd done that, God would send a fiery chariot to take his well-worn and faithful servant home.

This is a question about the here-and-now. It is not seeking an evaluation of the past, nor looking ahead to the vision of the future. It is earthed in reality: *what* are you really doing at the moment? It is a question which forces us to evaluate our ministry critically, to look at our priorities and motivations. It is uncomfortable, but crucial, if we wish to build for the future. A strategy for growth has to stand on solid rock not shifting sand. We need to pray that the Lord will 'speak through the earthquake, wind and fire' and that we may hear the 'still small voice of calm'.[35]

The individual context

What are we doing in terms of our individual lives? What 'added value' do we contribute in our workplace? What 'added value' do we give in our home, within our family? How real is your love for the Lord? How much fruit of the Spirit is seen in your life? The question is not, 'What experience do you have?' or 'How much do you earn?', important though those questions may be in other contexts. The Elijah question is 'What are you doing here, now?' How well do you really know your neighbours? How much service do you give in your home, and without being asked? Are your prayers real, or just a rushed duty each morning?

It is easy to look at such questions and grimace in despair. The purpose of them is not, however, to depress us, but to enable us to think strategically forward. One mission organization struggled for years to get its income above a static position; in desperation on one Strategy Day it was suggested that the topic for discussion should be 'Closure or Growth'. The experience of churches shown in Table 1.1 is that very few stable churches in an earlier period continued to be stable in a later period – just 2% of all churches, the lowest group. That is simply because stability is hard to hold – we either get worse or get better. Statisticians commonly say 'if present trends continue' and then make their predictions. The truth is that present trends rarely continue. It is equally true for us as individuals. It is hard to stay much as we are – we either take a determined step to change our priorities or we sink. Please be encouraged by the above questions to rethink your priorities if necessary.

As it is completely depressing and virtually impossible to move forward on all fronts at once, just choose one of these aspects (the most relevant to you) to work on initially, for example, your personal prayer time.

The institutional context

Elijah's question comes to organizations and churches as well. How strong is your advocacy programme, or your outreach programme? How real is the help you are giving to your beneficiaries? How deep is your worship? How good is your pastoral care? How effective is your team leadership? How great is your concern for the poor in reality? How much time is spent looking outwards? How much could you afford to be doing? Is your website really working?

Such questions enable you to explore the broad picture of your overall work. It is sometimes easy to look at a particular topic that is important – a new fund-raising appeal, or whether there should be a special mission meeting in the church – but it is sometimes worth doing a kind of overall audit of activities. What are the 5 or 8 key areas of work in which your agency or church is engaged? How many marks would you give each of them out of 10? Whichever is lowest on your list, why is that mark not as good as the others? Have you got your priorities right?

The headquarters of the Chelsea Building Society are in Tewkesbury, Gloucestershire. They were hit, like many other businesses, by the unexpected flooding of the town in 2007, and became desperate for clean water. They ordered a tanker of water from Dorset, hired a fire engine from Lincolnshire and appealed for help from the Fire Service College at Morton-in-Marsh to get fresh, clean water for their building.[36] Someone in leadership made clear decisions about priorities.

Gordon Graham was chairman of the publishers Butterworths for many years. He was a witty and eloquent speaker and at his retirement party he left his guests with a simple 5-point guide to the essentials of publishing.

- Only two really important things happen in a publishing house: the publishing decision and the sale.

- If you get one of them wrong, the other can still save you.

- If you get both of them wrong, you're dead.

- It's fun to visit the packing department, but you learn more in the returns department.

- Always run a company as if you were running for election on a losing ticket.[37]

Some of this wisdom could be applied to churches! The two really important things could be Worship and Conversions. The packing department is the home groups, and the returns department is pastoral visiting. Anglicans might translate the last item as running a church 'as if the church wardens were bringing a vote of no confidence at the AGM' and Baptists 'as if you were "preaching with a view" to a diaconate convinced the other candidate was better'.

Forgiven!

This is not a book on pastoral care, but sometimes in the process of evaluating where we are we can become conscious of the weight of past debris dragging us down.

Where we are now is influenced by that past bankruptcy, road accident or divorce.

I mentioned my involvement with the Kisumu orphanage earlier. One awful night, probably because she was suffering severe post-natal depression, the manager's wife either deliberately or accidentally caused an enormous fire with the paraffin she'd been using for cooking her husband's meal. The fire quickly caught hold and she and their 3 small children were burned to death. The other children in the Home were mercifully saved by the quick thinking of one of the dorm captains, a 19-year old lad waiting to go to college. That event was devastatingly traumatic for the manager, who was away at the time, and he had to forgive his wife for what had happened. Forgiving others, requesting forgiveness from others, and seeking reconciliation (as far as is possible) are often crucial for a person's wellbeing. Other, equally traumatic, examples are having to forgive a parent or grandparent for emotional or sexual abuse, or a father for walking out soon after you were born.

However, forgiving others, as we are bidden to do as Christians, in order that we ourselves may experience forgiveness, is sometimes not quite enough. We also have to be able to *forgive ourselves*, which can sometimes be even harder. We look back and realize how foolish we've been; if only we hadn't said this or done that. A minister of a thriving church committed adultery and had to resign his pastorate; his wife may have forgiven him, but he also had to forgive himself for doing something he had preached so vehemently against. R.T. Kendall, formerly of Westminster Chapel, wrote a book called *Total Forgiveness*, and especially stressed this need of self-forgiveness. Joseph may have forgiven his brothers for selling him as a slave to the Egyptians yet, even though he recognized that 'God sent me before you' (Gen. 45:7), he still had to forgive himself for his teenage arrogance (which had contributed towards turning his brothers against him).

The solution to forgiving ourselves is repentance and awareness of the enormity of our forgiveness by Christ. If we have truly experienced the awesome wonder of his forgiveness, how can we arrogantly hold on to our self-condemnation? The manager of the Kisumu Home had his fortieth birthday a few months after the fire. He deliberately took that occasion as a decisive moment for looking forwards and onwards, so that the burden of the past should not shackle him for ever. What are you doing here, right now? You may wish to jump up and shout, 'I'm forgiven!' Then you can go forward with enthusiasm and joy.

What are you doing here?

In order to give a properly thorough and comprehensive answer to this question it may be necessary to do an audit of one's work or personal life. This is like a financial audit but is based on activities and outcomes rather than just money.

Organizational audit

Suppose your team sits down and spends time completing a form like this:

Table 3.1: Organizational activities

Activity	Paid staff time per week	Volunteer staff time per week	Income for activity	Expenditure on activity	Percentage of available space occupied	Number of people involved	Effectiveness of ministry (out of 10)	Priority of this work

The activities might be the departments in an agency relating, for example, to outreach, communications, support and programme. You would need to assess criteria for 'effectiveness' in the final column. Some work, such as 'children's summer camp' for example, may take much time and effort, be given a relatively low effectiveness score but be judged of high priority.

A church could use a similar form and list its different Sunday and weekday activities. Some research has shown that, for example, while parents and toddlers groups in churches are common and reach many people, they are very ineffective in bringing new people into church.[38] If true for your church, you might decide, as one church did in our locality, to close down that activity as the space especially could be used in more productive ways which had a greater priority.

On the other hand, you may feel that immediate effectiveness is not a criterion which should determine priorities. For example, it may be years later when one of those parents or children, now teenagers, turns to your church for help, remembering the caring ministry of the group years earlier.

Individual audit

It is also important that, as an individual, you monitor your time use if you are going to attempt to prioritize your activities. One way of doing this is to construct a diary for a week with the hours broken down into half-hour slots, and then completing your major activity in each half-hour. It might look like Table 3.2 (if you get up before 6 a.m. or go to bed after 11.30 p.m. just add in the extra lines):

Table 3.2: Weekly diary for recording activities

	Sunday	Monday	Tuesday	Wednesday	Thursday	Friday	Saturday
6.00–6.30 a.m.							
6.30–7.00 a.m.							
7.00–7.30 a.m.							
…							
10.30–11.00 p.m.							
11.00–11.30 p.m.							

One Anglican minister kept a detailed record of how he spent his time in his church duties over several weeks.[39] If you have never done this you may well find it instructive. The results of his analysis were as follows:

Table 3.3: Time Breakdown of a Minister's Diary

ACTIVITY	% OF TOTAL TIME	AVERAGE NUMBER OF MINUTES PER OCCASION
Services	21	70
Home visits	20	40
Meetings	16	115
Study/preparation	15	85
Administration	12	240
Chaplain duties	8	125
Deanery duties	5	170
Magazine preparation	3	125
Total	100	105

This particular minister worked on average 53 hours a week, excluding meal breaks. Services included both Sunday and weekday services. Home visits related to pastoral visits, funeral or baptism preparations, home communions, and so on. Many types of meetings were necessary: social committee, youth group, the PCC, and meetings for stewardship, staff, worship, mission, local fraternal, ecumenical gathering and with the bishop. On average these lasted nearly 2 hours each. A sixth of his time was spent in meetings.

The value of such information is that it enables the broad parameters of duties to be assessed and evaluated. 'The trouble with time is that no one holds ministers accountable for it. They can wallow ineffectively day after day, their actions not really adding up to anything in particular, and no one notices.'[40] Noting what you do with your time helps to prevent such problems and also lays the basis for planning each week's work.

Knowing how much time each component takes on average also helps in determining priorities: what you should do today depends on how much free time you have. An American church leader, Carl George, said, 'There are two dangers for pastors: spending too much time getting ready for Sunday, and spending too little time.'[41] Balancing between an optimum quality of sermon and service and optimum involvement with people is essentially a priority problem. It is quite possible to spend too much time visiting people as well as too little: some evidence suggests that shorter visits can be more effective than longer ones.[42]

Gordon MacDonald, pastor and author, warns of spending too much time on VNPs (Very Nice People who are kind and sympathetic but who enjoy rather than share your passion) and VDPs (Very Draining People who sap our passion).[43] If you spend too much time with these two groups you ignore the VRPs (Very Resourceful People who ignite our passion), the VIPs (Very Important People who share our passion) and the VTPs (Very Trainable People who will catch our passion).

Your top priority

What, then, should we do first? One issue of the *Harvard Business Review* featured the story of an educational charity which assigned a young field worker to Peru.[44] He supervised the construction of schools in rural, hard-to-reach areas, and after two years had seen 200 new classrooms built at a very low cost. But when the directors of the agency came to visit him they found that neither literacy nor school attendance had improved. The young field worker was devastated – was his contribution to Peruvian education a total failure? What was the prime priority?

What is your prime priority? Here are three that you cannot delegate to anyone else, and for which you alone are responsible:

Your time with God. Whether you rise like Mother Teresa used to do at 4 a.m. each morning for Mass, spend time in daily devotions some other way, or regularly participate in Communion or other services, your relationship with God is your duty and no one else's. Others may encourage you, guide you, help you, pray with you, but ultimately your daily discipline of walking with God is yours alone and should include time alone with God as well as time with others in God's presence.

Your time with your family. Whether you are single or married, childless or a parent, old or young, part of your basic priority in life is to relate to your relations. In this context this means not just your spouse and children, but your brothers and sisters, parents and grandparents, aunts and uncles, cousins, nephews and nieces. No one else can take your place in your relationship with each of these: you alone are responsible.

Your time working out your vision. Your vision is precisely that – and not anyone else's. The Scriptures do not record anyone having the same vision twice (except perhaps Ezekiel by the River Chebar when he appears to see the throne of God in analogous ways in both chapters 1 and 10). You cannot delegate working out your vision. Although working at it may not consciously be a daily activity, it certainly ought to be reflected in your monthly and annual activities.

'What are you doing here?' suggests effective time management. That, in turn, relates to many things: setting goals; knowing your vision; dealing with interruptions; reading papers quickly; handling crises efficiently; long-term planning; motivation; evaluation; delegation and procrastination; and priorities – your top priority and your total priorities.

Your total priorities

Priorities relate to you as an individual. Your time with other people, your time with yourself, your time spent planning, your time with God, your time with your family, your time doing everything else are all aspects of your life. Time for yourself is specially important. A friend of mine once said, 'My husband was always wanting to talk with me. I found it frustrating as I never had space for myself.' People relax in different ways. What do you do: play golf or squash, walk, read, surf the web, collect stamps, do jigsaws? It does not matter, so long as you find some time in a busy week when you can really relax and enjoy what you do.

Priorities also relate to your work and your church. If you are a minister you need specially to keep a time for leisure, as your day off. A survey of senior ministers (Archdeacons) in 2003 found that only 50% of them took a day off – not a very good example to those for whom they were responsible.[45]

Resolving priorities is necessary in all three areas simultaneously: personal, work and church (or family or leisure). Each has its own triangle in this diagram, but the three triangles form a single triangle of priorities:

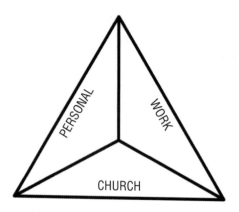

Sorting out your personal priorities in isolation can lead to disaster unless you organize all your priorities. One of the greatest difficulties Christians have in establishing priorities is understanding that we must deal with the whole man or woman. If we believe all our actions and opportunities are somehow related to the grand purposes of God, then all our life must reflect a consistent view. Personal goals – what we should do and what we should be – need to be considered alongside the work goals God has given us.[46]

You cannot have priorities unless you have goals to prioritize! Priorities need to be established to identify the order in which your goals should be undertaken and to fit into God's strategy as an effective servant. They reflect your basic value system. When the American baseball favourite, Yogi Berra, was asked to speak at a special father-and-son banquet, he gladly signed bats and balls given to him by the youngsters present until he noticed a group of lads who had no items for signing. Inquiring, he found they were from the local orphanage, and so he left the head table to talk with them and sign their programmes. When asked to return to speak he said, 'Go on with the programme. I am busy talking to my friends.'[47] Little things mean a lot.

The importance of sorting out priorities

Before we look at *how* to resolve priorities it is worth asking *why* we should do so. A 2008 advert had the strapline 'Let your business flourish in the future. Prepare for growth today.' If we do not sort out what we are doing here now, we will never sort out what we will become.

Is sorting out one's priorities too big a job? Walter Elliott once said, 'Perseverance is not a long race; it is many short races one after the other,' and priorities are exactly the same. A man was condemned to spend a night in a cell with a snake. The man was in one corner and the snake was in the other. All night long the man hardly dared to breathe for fear of alerting the snake, but when the morning light came, he saw it wasn't a snake at all but some old rope.[48] We can be fearful of reorganizing our life but find, if we have the courage to do so, that the problems we perceived to be there are nothing like as big as expected.

The large black church, Jesus House, led by Pastor Agu Irukwu, has a neat way of solving the issue of churchgoing for those who like to play golf on Sundays. It has a postcard which proclaims on top of a picture of a player 'Thank God for Sunday mornings' and then follows it up with the words 'It's great to catch up with your mates on the golf course on Sunday mornings . . . It'll be even greater when you pop into our new evening service afterwards. That way you can swing as the sun rises and sing as it sets.' You do not have to prioritize one over the other – just do both!

Resolving priorities

No one way of resolving priorities works in every situation, or with every person. The needs of others are different from yours perhaps, and your long-term needs will vary from those relating to the shorter term. Some priorities can be established on a single principle, others entail several simultaneously. These two aspects of complexity and time span will be used to identify four types of solution, as reflected in the following diagram:

	COMPLEXITY	
	Simple	Multiple
Shorter term	Basics	ABC
Longer term	80-20	Grid

Basic commitments (simple, shorter term)

This is a simple criterion which is relevant to shorter-term priority evaluations, although its roots are longer term. It is based on the three essential commitments that Christian people have, as summarized in this list:

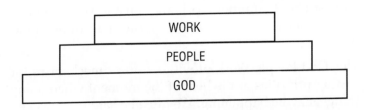

God. A personal encounter with Jesus Christ is fundamental for every true Christian believer. He determines our values and our actions. 'You are what you do, not what you believe.' The priority of that commitment to him as Lord needs to be reasserted every day.

People. When we come to Christ we find we have brothers and sisters we never ever thought of in the family of God. We did not choose each other. 'People' includes our times with our relations, times meeting others in the church, our times of socializing, of learning in home groups, and our service. We show our affiliation to the body of Christ and grow in our faith as we develop our spiritual relationships.

Work. If we are Christian 'professionals' this is usually defined as our paid work – a very limiting concept. If we work in a secular capacity it reflects our involvement with the programmes of our workplace and church. Pope John Paul II once said, 'Don't let the work of the Lord come before the Lord of the work.'

These three basic priorities give a simple order which can guide us. One day at Christian Research I had two letters, one from someone wanting work over the summer and one from someone wanting to know the number of Muslims in Wales. Both would require an answer but I only had time to do one that day. Which should I do? Putting people before work, I answered the request about summer work and left the Welsh figures for another day. People matter more than things (and numbers).

This God-People-Work provides a quick mechanism for sorting priorities in the heat of the moment when many things may be happening. We must be careful, however, not to let our desire to serve people interfere with the rest of the task. When the crowd came in acclamation to Jesus, he moved on to other towns to preach the kingdom of heaven there also. Although he frequently allowed people to interrupt his movements, he still kept to the purpose of his coming, a pattern for us to follow.

The 80-20 rule (simple, longer-term)

This concept was first described by a nineteenth-century economist called Pareto. It is essentially simple, even if geared for a long-term solution: what actions produce the greatest effect relatively?

The 'rule' means that 80% of your effectiveness comes from 20% of your activity, and therefore the remaining 20% of your effectiveness comes from 80% of your activity. The principle applies in many cases. For instance, 80% of a church's work is done by 20% of its members; 80% of an organization's donations come from

20% of its supporters; 80% of cars are made by 20% of the manufacturers; 80% of your problems come from 20% of your people, and 80% of your success or creativity comes from the few important decisions you make in the hour or so spent each day being specially productive.

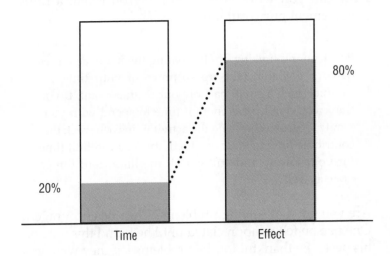

Although it is often called a 'rule', the implication of something so hard and fast is false. The numbers are approximate and may be 90-10 or 70-30 in some instances. It is the marked imbalance of two things which underlies the 'rule', not the precise definition.

In working out your priorities, it means that 80% of your effectiveness will come from using your key gifting. What is that? For some it is preaching, for others it is planning, or visiting, it may be creating new ideas, chairing meetings, evaluating, for others it is working relationally. The 80-20 rule is simply that whatever you are doing, do not neglect your primary gift, because your effectiveness (and image) are bound up with it. Do not move to a job where these primary skills have no room to flourish, or you will become intensely frustrated. Stay longer in a job where you have the opportunity to use them.

How can you work effectively? Myron Rush, a time management guru, put it this way

> Focus on minimizing or eliminating the many activities of your day that take up so much of your time yet produce such a small part of your overall result. If you think you don't have enough time to spend with your family, begin to eliminate the activities in each week that contribute little to your productivity. You can find time for your family and still get all the important things done as well.[49]

Are you good at solving problems? Then be encouraged. One person felt unappreciated until he found this note on his desk: 'Be thankful for the problems – if they were less difficult, someone with less ability would have your job.'[50]

The ABC technique (multiple, shorter-term)

This simple method for dealing with multiple activities can often be helpful for sorting out a mass of things to be done each day. At Christian Research, my long-suffering PA was asked to handle many items. 'Which should be done first, Peter?' she would say when overloaded. We frequently used this technique for resolving that question.

First make a list of the things you have to do. You can buy sheets already printed for this purpose, but the following takes only a minute to type on a computer:

Things To Do on . . . .

1 _____

2 _____

3 _____

4 _____

5 _____

6 _____

7 _____

8 _____

9 _____

10 _____

Some people prefer to write each task on a separate piece of paper which can then be thrown away when that task is done. The pieces of paper can always be reshuffled the next day to reflect changing priorities. But be careful. A Harry Martin cartoon shows a man sitting at a desk covered by notes of things he should be doing. A colleague is talking to him, and the seated man, says, 'Let me make a note of that. I can't do anything unless it is written down.' So much to do and all his time was spent in writing it down. But in truth, it is no laughing matter – we are fighting for time.

Having made such a list, check first that each is a proper goal, and then ask the following questions of each:

How urgent is it? Must it be done today? Or just soon? Or maybe sometime? (Can that magazine article not wait till tomorrow? May I not plan that next week?)

How important is it? Very important? (Yes, I'm out of cash, so I must go to the bank today.) What weight does the item have in your values? Are other people asking you to do something particularly important? (Yes, the regional minister wants this done this week.)

How often must this be done? Every day? Every week? Just occasionally? (That pastoral visit? Going to the dentist?)

Can someone else do this more effectively than I can? Often when the answer is 'yes' to this question we still do not hand it over because we greatly enjoy doing that particular job, perhaps because it requires a special knack to it, or an unusual skill. But delegating allows someone else to learn and gives you more time to do other things, including new things yourself.

Is it part of a larger task I am committed to? Will it contribute to your long-term goals? (If you want to be a mission worker in Brazil, it is sensible to spend time learning Portuguese.)

What will happen if it is not done at all? Will anyone notice? ('So you missed the choir practice!' How much does that really matter?) But some things not done, or done too late, can lead to disasters, like Chernobyl.

Having amended the list in the light of the answers to such questions, deleting or amending as necessary, what then? Go through the items looking for those which are of greatest importance or highest value and mark them

A. Then go through and mark items which are not important and have a low value with a C rating. All those which are then not marked A or C must be B: things you should do, are fairly important and have medium value.

Frequently in such an exercise too many activities get labelled A. Go through these and label them AA, AC or AB. Your priorities then are to follow – in order – the AA tasks, and when completed the AB tasks, then the AC, and if there is any time left over the B tasks, and the C tasks. Tomorrow, repeat the exercise but re-categorize the priorities according to any change in circumstances.

Here is a hypothetical example of how this might work, taken from one of the many PPP (Priorities, Planning and Paperwork) seminars I have had the privilege to lead.

1	Visit 3 nearby families this week who don't go to church	A	AA
2	Preach on the subject of world mission at least twice in next 6 months	B	
3	Prepare my next 2 sermons with 24 hours to spare	A	AC
4	Restrict my committee membership to 5	B	
5	Lead a party to the Holy Land next year	A	AC
6	Enrol on a rapid reading course by the end of the month	C	
7	Spend extra 15 minutes in prayer every Monday for next 3 months	A	AA
8	Move to a larger church in 3 years' time	C	
9	Phone or email my brother every 2 weeks for next 6 months	B	
10	Read a chapter of a book on leadership every day for the next month	A	AB

The priorities are:
> Visiting
> Praying
> Reading
> Preparing
> Leading
> Preaching
> Restricting
> Phoning

One rarely has time to do the Cs. Write down now the things that you have to do tomorrow large or small (using the list of 10 blank lines given earlier if you wish) and identify your A priorities, then your Cs and Bs. Repeat with As if necessary. Now follow the order shown. That is what prioritization is all about. But do one thing at a time. Lord Chesterfield wrote to his son in 1747, 'There is time enough for everything in the course of the day if you do but one thing at once; but there is not time enough in the year if you will do two things at a time.'

Basics: The urgent and the important (multiple, longer-term)

Ultimately priorities focus on two areas – time and value. How quickly must something be done? How important is it? The answers to these two questions provide virtually all the directions to a person's priorities. Eisenhower is reputed to have said, 'I make sure that only the urgent and the important cross my desk.' To help think through such answers a four-box grid on these two aspects is given below, with each area broken into two parts.

URGENCY

		Low	High
I M P O R T A N C E	Low	D	C
	High	B	A

Box A indicates an activity which is both highly urgent for you and personally very important. It has to be done quickly and done correctly, as far as you are concerned. What should your reaction be? Easy: *do it at once,* or at least schedule it for immediate action.

Box B indicates that something is personally highly important but does not have to be done immediately. What then do you do? *You plan it!* The need for personal planning arises when you want to be sure something goes as well as it can and you have time on your side. One of the personal priorities mentioned above was 'your time spent planning'. It is crucial that every agency and church leader puts time aside, perhaps two or three days a month, to plan the way ahead, whether short-term assignments such as next month's services, or longer-term objectives and goals for the coming year. In an article on time management in *Reader's Digest,* Sue Walsh, co-founder of WorkLife Architect, puts as the first of 15 tips 'Give yourself thinking time.'[51]

Box D reflects an action which, as far as you are concerned, is not important and has no urgency attached to it. What should you do? *Forget it!* Or at least, forget it for the moment. Why spend your time doing something which does not matter and which can be done any time?

This kind of approach is, of course, fairly rigid. It doesn't take into account the pressure often caused by the need to fulfil targets within a presumed timescale, gives no leeway for God-given interruptions such as that phone call or visit from someone in real need, or the sense of failure if targets are not met, etc.

Delegation

The box labelled C represents a task that has to be done quickly but is not critically important to you personally. Where you have someone available, therefore, the best action is to *delegate* it. For those in an office or management structure in a Christian organization, delegation may be relatively easy. For many ministers, especially those working with several churches, it is not so simple. But part of the function of a church is to help its members to grow, and people have the opportunity of growth as they are encouraged to take action. You may need to persuade somebody to try something, you may need to teach them how to do it, but eventually delegation saves you effort – and you have taken one step further in the process of building your team. Patience and understanding are two of the disciplines of delegation. Always delegate things you cannot do. *Invariably* delegate things which are not part of your primary goals, tasks or priorities.[52]

The art of delegation was summarized as a series of dos and don'ts in a book published more than 50 years ago, but is still as relevant today as when it was first written.[53] They are

Delegating IS	Delegating IS NOT
Giving to others responsibility for a task, and thus some authority	Telling others to do what they are told to do
Helping others get the skills they need to accomplish the task	Assuming all facets of the task are initially understood
Understanding the problems felt in coping with the responsibility	Listening to excuses as to why the job has not been done
Matching potential with opportunity to grow	Giving duties to people way beyond their capability
Trusting others to get better with experience, and so share in the decision-making process	Wishing you had done the job in the first place
Ensuring you show a person both why and how it is to be accomplished	Concluding that you were stupid to give that job to that person
Allowing errors to be made in a learning environment, giving freedom for acting as thought fit	Pointing out all the mistakes a person has made in doing a job

Towards the vision

Most of the activities you will do as an individual and that your church or agency does will be located in Box A (this was also mentioned in chapter 1 but is so important to be worth repeating). In fact, so much goes into Box A that it gets overcrowded and the elements in it need to be broken down one stage further, as shown in the diagram below (the same as Table 1.2)

HIGH IMPORTANCE	HIGH URGENCY		
		Short-term	Long-term
	Minor	Z	Y
	Major	Y	X

Looking at the A activities in this way is equivalent to categorizing them AA, AB or AC in the previous system. Completing these boxes forces answers to the questions of time and value, not now in terms of whether the activity is essential or non-essential, but of how crucial it is. Box X items are usually easier to distinguish, and it can be argued about which of the two Box Ys is the most important. Box Z in this context is least important, though still valued enough to be there.

There is a progression therefore from Box X to Boxes Y to Box Z. Critical action tends to focus on Box X: your basic priorities as a church or organization or individual are driven by activities of high long-term urgency and of major importance. That is precisely how it should be.

What are you doing here? Activities X, Y and Z. The crucial Box X actually has another name – it is also called 'Your Vision', and we shall now turn to defining that.

A former Bishop of Guildford, the Rt Revd Michael Adie, once said there were three kinds of clergy (and his comments are equally true of non-Anglican ministers and those in other professions):

- Those who are obviously busy;
- Those who are not obviously busy; and
- Those who are obviously not busy.

It is only those in the second category, he went on to say, who will fulfil their vision. Somehow we have to stop the imperative of the urgent and make time to plan the important. Only those with sufficient self-discipline to do that are likely to achieve their vision.

4

WHAT DO YOU SEE?

This is an *incisive* question. God asks it of at least three prophets in the Bible: Jeremiah, Amos, Zechariah and, interestingly, he asks it of each of them twice. With Jeremiah, it was in the context of his call to service and the answers given, 'a branch of an almond tree' and 'a boiling pot' (Jer. 1:11,13), were specific, concrete items.

Likewise to Amos, in the context of his prophetic messages to a reluctant Israel, who gave the answers 'a plumb-line' and 'a basket of summer fruit', again both concrete items with allegorical meanings (7:8; 8:2).

And with Zechariah: in his visions he was asked what he saw and he replied, 'a lampstand all of gold' and 'a flying scroll', both of which are particular objects, even if a little unusual (Zech. 4:2; 5:2).

Each of these prophets could have given broad measurements of the objects they saw – tall, wide or long. Presumably they could have given the colours of the objects also. They would be describing physical and familiar things with which they and God were concerned. Jeremiah was commended by God for his reply, 'You have seen well', for the objects he saw were of coming judgement. The two objects Amos saw were also linked to a coming judgement. One of Zechariah's prophecies on the other hand was linked to the hope of building a new Temple when the 70-year captivity in Babylon had ended, although the other was linked to the curse of the social sins of his day.

Time-wise, Amos was the earliest of these three, prophesying while there were still the two countries of Israel and Judah, before the former was swallowed up by Assyria capturing its capital, Samaria, in 721 BC. Jeremiah prophesied at the end-times for the country of Judah and saw it defeated by Nebuchadnezzar and the people taken into captivity to Babylon in 586 BC. Zechariah came after Jeremiah and helped to inspire the rebuilding of the Temple about 520 BC. God therefore asks his servants what they saw during periods of stress, disaster and freedom, that is, very roughly, whatever kinds of circumstances we ourselves might be in.

The people God spoke to were leaders but outside the main line of the priestly hierarchy. They brought specific messages at particular times based on the data which they had evaluated (and as guided by God). They told God what they saw, but they needed to ask him for an explanation of what the objects meant, and proceeded to give that understanding to their hearers, drawing out the implications for action that were necessary. It would seem that the objects these prophets saw were each used as the basis for several sermons.

'What do you see?' therefore is a question which has implications for the future in some way, a future which in these examples stretches from 2 or 3 years ahead (Zechariah and the new Temple) to effectively a lifetime of perhaps 30 or 40 years for Jeremiah, with Amos somewhere in between at perhaps 10 years ahead. When Jesus says to his disciples of the (third) Temple, 'You see all these, do you not?', he foretold its destruction in the next 40 years (Matt. 24:2).

Thus the question, when asked in the Scriptures, seems to suggest answers which are specific (that is, measurable in some way), futuristic (in the immediate and not very long-term), and in circumstances that might apply in any age. Because they are all future-orientated, we could describe this as a visionary question, since it is precisely these characteristics which need to be used for understanding the visions we might have in our day and age. A much wider overview of 'vision' and the Bible has been given elsewhere.[54]

There is one other feature which may be taken from the six references cited. In five of them (all except one in Zechariah) the breadth of the vision might be described as 'national', possibly 'global'. Tearfund's 2008 advert asking people to join them in 'relieving poverty for 100 million people through 100,000 churches worldwide over the next 10 years' is an example of such a wide-ranging vision.

In the sixth (building the new Temple) the vision might be described as 'local'. When the exiled Israelites finally returned to their land a huge number of things had to be done to ensure they once again became a living, operational country. The new Temple was extremely important for this process, but only one of the major reconstruction jobs to be undertaken.

Some of our visions might be 'national' and a number of those made public often are, like the prophecy before the death of Diana, Princess of Wales, of a time of national mourning expressed with flowers in the cities.[55] For the rest of this chapter, however, we will focus on 'local' visions, relevant for the individual person, agency or church.

Personal vision

What would you like to be doing in 10 years' time? One of the leaders of life-work planning, John Crystal, says,

'You don't start out saying, "I need a job", you start by asking, "What do I want to do with my life?"' In his book, *Re-inventing the Corporation*, Naisbitt quotes career consultant Buck Blessing as saying, 'The most difficult person to manage is the person who has no idea what he or she wants to do',[56] something that many people can verify from experience. Such people are heading nowhere and seem to arrive where they're headed!

I like the story of three workmen building St Paul's Cathedral. They were each asked what they were doing. The first answered, 'I'm chipping this stone.' The second replied, 'I'm cutting this block to fit into that corner.' The third lifted his head high with dignity and stated, 'I'm helping Sir Christopher Wren build a cathedral.'[57]

William Carey, the father of modern missions, said

> Expect great things from God,
> Attempt great things for God.[58]

It is easy to repeat his words, but much harder to ask ourselves what we are actually expecting from God, or, perhaps even more difficult, what are we actually attempting for God. Next time you go for a walk tease out answers to such thoughts.

How do we find our vision? Partly through reading the Scriptures, partly through prayer, sometimes through dreams, often through receiving information or data, maybe through your personal experiences, through understanding your gifts and skills, and ascertaining what is at hand. 'You need to be able to imagine that the future can improve upon the present if you want to achieve anything at all,' says writer and musician James Williams.[59]

You are what you have been becoming. Your past with all its heredity and development has helped to fashion you as you are now. But the question is not now 'Where are you?' or 'What are you doing here?' but 'What do you see . . . yourself becoming?' What, where, who will you be in 10 years' time?

Fancy Jesus calling a despised tax-collector like Matthew to become one of his disciples! But he had the vision of what Matthew could become. On the line below, write today's date. Now alter the year to make it five years from today. Conscious of the proverb 'Trust in the LORD with all your heart, and do not rely on your own insight. In all your ways acknowledge him, and he will make straight your paths' (Prov. 3:5–6), write down what you see yourself becoming by that date:

_____

If 5 years is too short a timescale, try answering instead, 'What will I have become by the time I retire?' When James Dobson's father died they found that in his will he requested the words 'He prayed' be put after his name on his tombstone. There are some 80,000 verbs in the English language. Which would you choose for your life? He preached, she served, he cared, he helped, she loved, she enabled, she made, he built . . . ? On the drawing, put first your name, and then write your epitaph on the bottom two lines.

No-one is suggesting this is a quick or easy process, but long-term planning necessitates knowing what you want to accomplish. This is the heart of vision building. Wrestle with it, pray over it, beseech the Lord to guide you in sufficient self-knowledge to know what you might accomplish for him. Bill Hybels has written a book called *Holy Discontent* exploring this process. Elsewhere I have written how I struggled to find my own vision, until at last it came: 'He counted for God.'[60] When I retired from Christian Research, the then Chairman, Paul Sandham, gave me a bronze plate on which was inscribed 'Peter counts for God July 2007', which was much appreciated. I hope I still do when I meet the Lord face to face.

Corporate vision

How can institutions, organizations or churches find a vision? Are there ways, for example, in which local churches can help combat declining numbers by increasing the energy, the enthusiasm, the effort and the excitement in churchgoing?[61] In *Pulling out of the Nosedive* the first of five challenges to churches is doubling their congregation in 5 years. If every person brought a friend that could be done.

In a series of seminars called 'How Not to Have a Pear-Shaped Church', delegates were challenged to say what they would do in the next 3 months if they were going to attempt to double their congregation in 5 years.

Although many of those present said it was an impossible vision, when asked to think strategically about how it might be accomplished, some very sensible answers were forthcoming, including:

- Engage with the community

- Drop some activities

- Have more positive preaching and teaching

- Employ a youth worker

- Encourage 'back to church . . .'

- Build on contacts already available, e.g. schools

- Find more space

- Plan joint evangelistic activities

- Encourage people to pray for those known to them

- Use the more relational people better.[62]

Formulating a vision

How can you go about formulating a vision for your agency, business or church? The answer is in one of two broad ways. Strategic thinking is either thinking forward to the future based on the past and present or thinking backwards from the more distant future to the nearer future. I know both methods produce effective results as I have had the privilege of leading dozens of groups in 'Vision Building Days' using whichever approach the leader or the minister felt was most suitable.

The first method is illustrated by this drawing of a cricketer who has just been bowled out. He dislikes that state of affairs and is saying that if he is given another chance someday of batting again, and he is bowled the same type of ball that he has just had, he will play a different kind of stroke in order to avoid the same outcome. That is what many of us would call common sense, but in reality what he is doing is planning forwards from his current, negative performance. It is a perfectly valid way of approaching the future.

Planning forward from current performance

If an organization has seen its income increase 5% over the last 2 years, it is quite legitimate for it to say, 'Let's see if we can increase it again by another 5% over the next 2 years.' Or if a church has seen its congregation grow from 50 to 70 in a year, it is worth seeing if they can help it to increase from 70 to 90 in the next year.

Planning back from the future

The second way of thinking is demonstrated by the second drawing in which a cricketer has come to the last ball of the over. Bowling will then be from the other end. The cricketer, keen to make a century, and therefore desiring as many runs as possible, knows he can only score runs if he faces the bowler. Hence if he scores just one run off the next ball, he will be at the other wicket, ready to face the new bowler when he bowls from the other end. His immediate actions are being shaped by his desire to reach a future target. He is planning backwards from the desired outcome, and this affects his immediate actions.

These two ways of strategic thinking are called here respectively 'vision building' and 'Horizon Mission

Methodology' and will each be described in more
detail.[63] It should be noted, however, that they have some
common features:

- They are *personal*, that is, they usually come to just one
  individual who then shares it with others. Virtually
  all the visions in the Scriptures come to a single
  person, the prime mover.

- They are *clear*. The vision can be talked about. It is
  specific. People know what it is you are hoping to do.
  In the 1980s my brother's vision was 'to buy a
  narrowboat so that the less privileged children of
  Lewisham could have the opportunity of a holiday
  and see the countryside'. Everyone knew what he
  meant. He achieved it with much hard work,
  eventually seeing three narrowboats commissioned.

- They are *shareable*. The vision may come to an
  individual but it must be shared with others. For
  leaders to be followed, their vision must be
  communicated.

- They are *realistic*. A vision invariably builds upon and
  uses your gifts. God builds on our previous experience
  of walking with him, and our past understanding of
  him, and then moves us on to new levels of revelation.

- They are *energizing*. Energy motivates. Nothing
  significant for God was ever accomplished without
  energy. David Wilkerson, founding pastor of the Times
  Square Church in New York, said one Sunday a few
  years ago in his sermon 'I'm 72, and I have energy'
  and went on to call for 100 under-25 volunteers to go
  overseas with the message of Christ. Several hundred
  responded.[64]

Vision building

Vision building is about building a vision, that is, it is looking forwards, seeing ahead to a new or different situation. A seesaw without a fulcrum in the middle would just be a flat plank; with one, however, it becomes great fun for children. Likewise, your vision is the vital fulcrum that holds strategy and guiding principles together. The principles give the framework for the endeavour, the vision gives the future picture and the strategy is the way of fulfilling it. The ten commandments were the principles, 'the land flowing with milk and honey' was the vision, the conquering settlement by the tribes of Israel the fulfilment. The vision was central and crucial – without it the Israelites would never have got there, although of course it also depended on God's faithfulness to his covenant promise with Abraham.

Four questions

This method of thinking strategically focuses around four questions, the second of which has already been considered in the previous chapter.

Purpose ➡	Why are you here?
Mission ➡	What are you doing?
Vision ➡	What will you become?
Thrusts ➡	How will you do it?

The first three of these questions are time related. The first, purpose, looks to the past. The second, mission, looks to the present. The third, vision, looks to the future. This method of strategic thinking recognizes where you have come from, in order to work out where you hope to go.

Purpose: Why are you here?

Where you have come from can be important for your future. Never dismiss the traditions you inherit; sometimes they can be very significant. A church founded to serve deaf people, for example, will probably always see that as its prime ministry; the original purpose continues into the future even if the methods used change greatly.

Answering the question 'Why are you here?' or 'Why was your church started?' is usually fairly easy. Here are three purpose statements taken from the *Tyne and Wear Christian Directory* which show, like most purpose statements, that they haven't changed across the subsequent years:

> Christ Church, Gateshead: Anglican presence in the inner city.
>
> St Agnes Roman Catholic Church, Gateshead: to serve the spiritual needs of the parishioners in Crawcrook and surrounding areas.
>
> Whitburn Methodist, South Tyneside: a village chapel forming a nucleus for wider sharing.

This is not to say that purpose statements never change, but if they do it is likely to be after a considerable time, perhaps 50 or 100 years. Nor are the statements given above in order for them to be critiqued; they are the words of the minister who answered the question at the time. They each make a statement about their church, and each, as it happens, is very different – a presence, a service and a nucleus. Each will bring with them their own context for working out that purpose and their own culture also. The outworking will change over time, and so probably will the culture, but, if the church wishes, the purpose remains supreme.

As already mentioned in chapter 1, when a similar question was asked of Anglican Kenyan churches in a seminar, answers were very different, reflecting a totally dissimilar culture:

- To reach out in evangelism
- To ease administration
- To resolve conflict
- To provide a church closer for elderly people
- To deal with church politics.

Here are three examples of organizational purpose statements which are publicly available.

Chartered Institute of Management: to promote the development and successful exercise of management skills.

Urban Saints: to release an army of radical young people who are committed to taking the Gospel to the generations who don't know Jesus Christ.

Mothers' Union: to be specially concerned with all that strengthens and preserves marriage and Christian family life.

All these examples of purpose statements begin with an infinitive, that is, a verb beginning with the word 'to'. An infinitive states a purpose without involving people in the definition of that purpose, even if people are essential for its fulfilment. This means that such statements are crisp, detached and have, well, a sense of purpose!

Why do you exist?

This is a close but a sufficiently different alternative question to arrive at a similar answer. Charles Handy, the management guru, suggests using this question to help in identifying your purpose. He gives some examples from well-known companies:

Walt Disney: To make people happy.

Wal-Mart: To give ordinary folk the chance to buy the same things as rich people.

Merck: To preserve and improve human life.

These statements can be made to fit changing circumstances. For example, your church may have been started 'to fulfil a need on a new estate'. Over time the estate will no longer be new and the needs will be different, but the original purpose remains true.

How can you identify your purpose?

In practice, how does your church or organization work out its purpose?

- Have a discussion amongst the senior leadership team, and ask each to write down their answer to the question, 'Why are we here?' or 'Why do we exist?'

- By looking at the common elements in the answers see if you can formulate a statement, beginning with the word 'to'.

- When you have a finished statement, share it with others and note their reactions. If necessary, make further changes.

- In 6 months' time return to it, making any further adjustments to the wording or the concepts. Then make it public on your letterhead or magazine.

There are times when it is essential to know why an organization exists. On one occasion I was asked to lead a Vision Building Day for a well-known Christian organization. As part of the process I split the executive leadership team (about 12 people) into two groups and asked each to write down what the purpose of their organization was, expecting to get two broadly similar statements with different wording. We would then jointly agree a combined statement. To my surprise and theirs, they came up with two different and contradictory statements. We spent the next two hours trying to work out which statement, or which new statement, did reflect that organization's *raison d'etre*. Unless you know what you are here for, it's a bit difficult trying to achieve it.

Mission: What are you doing?

Two organizations may have a similar purpose but differing missions. Thus Oxfam and Christian Aid both have as their purpose the alleviation of suffering through relief and development worldwide. Oxfam deals with this largely in a participative manner (by organizing actions at local level, bringing in extra staff and resources as necessary directly) whereas Christian Aid handles its work mostly in a non-participative manner by providing resources (usually finance) to organizations already in a position in a country to handle the needs.

A single organization may have more than one distinct mission, like Statistics Finland, the National Statistics Office of Finland, whose mission is:

1) Helping citizens form a reliable picture of society,

2) Aiding Government and corporate decision making, and

3) Creating conditions for social and economic research.[65]

Mission statements all explain what the organization or church is doing NOW, that is to say, they need to be phrased in the present. One way of ensuring this is to phrase them so that the first word is a verb which ends in '-ing'. The above example does this. Here are three others, all examples from churches:

Ebenezer Church, Tyneside (Christian Brethren): providing regular family worship, Bible-based teaching and preaching of the gospel.

St Luke's Church, Bath (Anglican): making Christ known in our communities.[66]

URC Church, North London: providing a centre for worship, and facilities for the local community.

(Please see chapter 3 also for an exploration of mission.)

Vision: What will you become?

What is vision? At its simplest it is a statement about the future. The travel guide firm Frommers ran a good series of advertisements in the mid-1990s. 'Know where you're going before you get there' was their strap line, and they expected you to buy their guide to Nepal, say, before your visit. The assumption was that you knew you were going to Nepal, not just 'going somewhere on holiday'. However, the punch line could also relate to time generally, and might be translated, 'Know your vision so that you can state where you are headed.'

'Vision,' says George Verwer, who began the mission literature agency Operation Mobilisation in 1964 and has seen it grow worldwide and diversify since, 'is a powerful sense of what needs to be done and the initiative to take hold of it and work towards its completion'.[67] As someone else said, 'the way to know if a vision is from God is that it will be something you can't do'.[68] Determining your vision, or the vision of your church or organization means thinking ahead. What will be different as a consequence of your work in 10 years' time?

Some say vision has to be inspiring, challenging, creative and revealed. It certainly helps if it is! But I am not sure that it has to be such. Vision is a firm, future destination to which both you and your organization are clearly travelling.

The importance of the vision looking to the future cannot be overstated. One church's statement was 'To help people recognize the presence of God in their daily lives and relationships'. This is a worthy objective, and doubtless challenging. But it is not vision; it is a statement of current intentions and activity. It is in fact a mission statement and would have been better expressed 'Helping people recognize . . .'. Be sure your 'vision' has a future implication.

Some leaders do not think of themselves as having vision, yet they demonstrate it in their ministry. Several of the church leaders in *Back from the Brink* did not want to be described as 'visionaries', yet they believed that things could be different in the church for which they were responsible. They took positive action, and each turned around a church which had been about to close.[69] Surely this is vision, whatever the person concerned may call it.

Testing your statement

Management Futures is a forward looking business dedicated to giving the best counselling and management training, using twenty-first-century techniques. Its two founding directors were both BBC Heads of Department. It suggests that vision statements should get positive answers to the following questions.

- Is it short and simple?
- Is it inspiring?
- Does it describe what you uniquely do?
- Could your staff say what it is? [or congregation]
- Could your most junior staff say what it is? [or newcomers]
- Are you using it to measure your performance?
- Have you revisited it in the last two years?[70]

Not all the above examples (those quoted previously under 'Mission: What are you doing?') would get seven positive answers to these questions. They suggest using the vision statement as something by which to measure performance, but not all do so. If they do, you will know whether or not you have achieved what you set out to accomplish. Three measurable church vision statements are:

URC Church, North London: To increase support to young families, so they become 40% of our attendance in 5 years' time.

Rhema Church, Johannesburg, South Africa: To build a church community of 25,000 in 15 years. (This was stated in 1984, and they had fulfilled it by the mid-1990s, ahead of schedule, so they are now aiming to build a church community of 50,000 by 2010, and have already enlarged the church to seat 8,000 at a single service.)

Emmanuel Church, south-west London: By 2000, we will be an attractive, worshipping fellowship . . . so that those linked to the church will number about 1,000. (It took slightly longer than anticipated, but by 2008, they had 3 services every Sunday with 400 plus people in each.[71])

But not all visions are directly measurable. They then run the danger of becoming more diffuse, lacking crispness, but that doesn't mean they are incorrect or unworkable. Not at all! Some such vision statements are:

St Andrew's, Eastcote: To so communicate the excitement and joy of the message Jesus taught that people will gladly respond.

Salesian Sisters of St John Bosco: To allow others to capture responsible, caring, challenging and enthusiastic leadership roles.

Handbag.com: To be the most useful site online for women.[72]

Market Research Society: To be an organization that reflects an exciting and forward-looking industry.[73]

The impact of vision

True visions make a difference. They impact our personal world; we are never quite the same again once we have determined what it is we are aiming to do. It impacts our *learning* – we now read certain books, look at appropriate websites, buy relevant videos, go on particular courses. It impacts our *resources* – we are now saving to build an extension, or send someone to Africa, or collecting clothing to give to needy asylum seekers. It impacts our *relationships* – we need to get to know special groups of people, approach certain officials, write to relevant leaders. It can impact our *structures* – if it does, this is usually in a radical way: we have to be properly organized so as to deliver the goods. It impacts our *image* – we are now seen to be people with a message, a driven group perhaps, but those wanting to make a difference.

How do we get our vision?

There is no single or simple way. It will probably need to involve many of the following.

• Personal and corporate *prayer*, asking God for guidance, wisdom and revelation.

- Intensive *discussion* within the leadership team. This can sometimes be helped by an external facilitator.

- Reckon on taking a full day at least, after much prayer, preparation and preliminary discussion. What do you feel God would like you to become in 5 years' time? Ask people to write their answer on a Post-it Note, then put them all up and read what each has said. What are the *common threads*? You may well be able to identify three, four or even more items of importance.

- Sometimes there is another step. What if there are significant differences of opinion in your team, or no-one else supports the main thing you believe is right? There needs to be a time for negotiation, prayer, analysis of motives and much discussion, but you may not be able to get a specific statement (see next item) until disagreements are resolved in some way. For example, if you are a new mission-minded minister in an introspective church, it may take months of teaching before people are ready to consider looking outwards.

- Then comes the crucial part. Imagine yourself in a helicopter looking down on these five or so items. Can you find a wider yet *specific statement* which embraces either all of them or the majority? Are some included within others if certain ones are adopted? Go for a wider context, a broader view, an overarching formula.

- *Return* to it on a future occasion as you may not achieve *agreement* initially. It has to be worked through. No-one said strategic thinking was easy. But it is out of such deep yearnings and struggles that the vision comes.

And then what? For nearly 30 years, till it was taken out of service in October 2003, Concorde sped between New York and London in three and a quarter hours at a speed of Mach 2, twice the speed of sound. To do that its throttle was always fully open: it constantly flew flat out. So must we, once our vision is known. Benjamin Disraeli once said, 'The secret of success is constancy of purpose'. A letter I received from George Verwer is signed 'Keep on keeping on!'

There is another facet here also. Some have suggested that vision and its visualization lead *to* belief, as well as, or instead of, stemming *from* belief.[74] Creating something that looks beautiful (like Concorde) or watching a play that touches your emotions deeply often enables you to see, literally or intuitively, something which is bigger or better, helping to form a belief that a vision is possible or desirable. This has been called 'the witness of excellent practice' and it is, of itself, a testimony to the grace and power of God. Someone once said of one of Saltmine's theatrical performances that they are 'remarkable in their ability to communicate creatively'.[75] Saltmine, an evangelistic agency based in Dudley, wants to launch a children's theatre company *Slingshot* by 2010, hoping that through being a 'witness of excellent practice' belief may come – in this case in Jesus Christ.

Thrusts

The fourth question given under 'vision building' was 'How will you do it?' Successful planning is crucially important for the adequate fulfilment of vision. There are many books on this subject, however, and so the topic of planning is not dealt with here at length.[76] 'The path is not the destination; Emerson said that where you are on the path is not nearly as important as the direction you are facing.[77]

Malcolm Macdonald is the vicar of St Barnabas, Kensington. A few years ago the church's vision was big and simple: to help '1,000 children at risk'. How did they do it? What were their 'thrusts'? They contacted each of their mission workers overseas involved with children. They all worked together that year, alongside other ministries, while the home church prayed, gave, sent some for short-term involvement, and supported specific projects. 2,700 children were impacted that year across 7 countries in some physical or spiritual way.[78]

Nicky Gumbel of Holy Trinity Brompton (HTB), preached on vision one Sunday in 2007. He called it 'The sign on the bus'. He explained that HTB's vision had six elements. It was to see:

- Millions of people come to know Jesus Christ
- The churches in the UK filled again to capacity
- The divorce rate falling and marriage and family life built up
- The prison population falling
- An end to extreme, unnecessary poverty and people dying of preventable diseases
- Every child in the world have a universal primary education.

In order to accomplish this he urged the congregation to do 3 things (the 'thrusts'):

- Get on board the bus ('on this bus everyone has something to do')

- Gear up (grow spiritually, serving as you grow)

- Go for it in love.[79]

A church in Cricklade, Wiltshire, had a Vision Building Day recently. Did it work? That day a number of areas for development were identified. Eight months later they reported:

- Outreach: setting up a strategy group; producing a leaflet for distribution at the town fair; special Sunday service showing an evangelistic DVD; asking the local theatre to perform an evangelistic production; setting up a website team.

- Youth: setting up a joint church strategy group; thinking about appointing an ecumenical youth worker.

- Leadership: Army Chaplain from Fiji on temporary duty to liven up worship; worship group organizes a service every 6 weeks (once a month was too much); continuing to use drama in church services; celebrating birthdays once a month.

- Relevance: focussing on a new minister who was due to start in two months' time.[80]

Each of these thrusts was carefully thought through. Vision building works!

Horizon Mission Methodology

At a NASA meeting in the nineties someone is said to have asked, 'What will the world be like in 2100?'

Someone replied, 'People will be living on Mars then.'

'I'm not sure about that,' responded someone else.

A new voice entered the discussion, 'Let's not worry for the moment whether it is true. Let us assume that people will be living on Mars in 2100. What do we have to do between 2000 and 2010 to ensure that it comes true?' And that is the vital breakthrough question! It assumes that the vision is worthwhile and obtainable.

In terms of most businesses, agencies and churches the NASA timescale of 2100 is far too long, roughly ninety years ahead. Unless we are NASA, or Shell looking for oil deposits, most of our timescales are set at 5 or 10 years ahead, 20 years at the most. The Tomorrow Project is one of the few organizations deliberately seeking to look 20 years ahead. Its first publication in May 2000, subtitled 'using the future to understand the present', gave various scenarios over the years 2000 to 2020 (see bibliography under Michael Moynagh).

The essence of NASA's question, however, is still relevant. It is quite possible to rephrase it, 'If your church or organization is to become like X [the equivalent of a person on Mars] in 10 years' time, what does it have to do in the next year?' ('10 years' and 'year' can be any convenient periods of time.)

The discussion at NASA was clearly stimulating. Subsequently a paper was written for *Futures Quarterly*[81] which propounded Horizon Missions Methodology, and this technique has since gone under that name, usually abbreviated for convenience to just HMM.

The essence of the technique is:

- To imagine the future as a doorway, part of which can be seen by looking through a peep-hole in the doorway of the present.

- To imagine you are at the future doorway, and looking through a peep-hole in that door *back* towards the present doorway.

- To imagine that what you then see in the present doorway is in fact an expanded field of present knowledge.

This may be illustrated as follows, taken from the *Futures Quarterly* article:[82]

Figure 4.1: Graphic Depiction of HMM

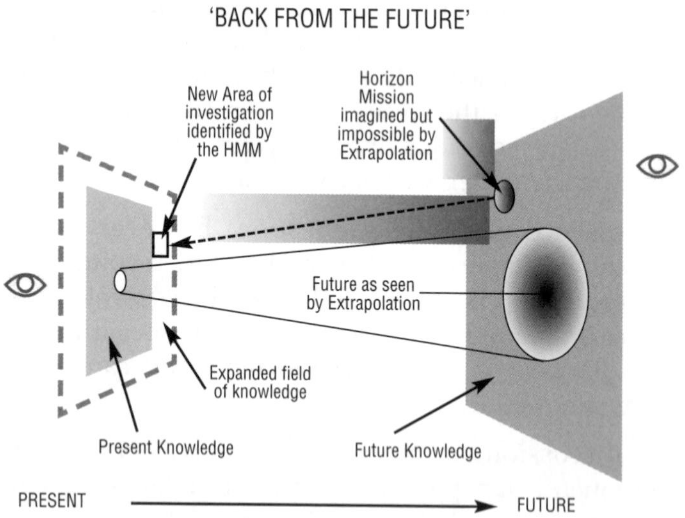

'BACK FROM THE FUTURE'

These 'imaginations' provide the second means of strategic thinking. In effect it is to look at the future, not by extrapolating from the past and present (as vision building did) but by coming back to the near future from the viewpoint of the distant future. It is an interesting process, which works!

Values

Horizon Mission Methodology makes the key assumption that the values driving people in a church or society transposed into the future will be the same as the values those identical people have in the church or society today. This is a reasonable assumption, since it is the same people involved in both time frames. We are not asking what will the values be in society in say 50 years' time, but what are the values of present day people if they were time-travelled to 50 years' hence?

A research project reported in 2006 by Community Links looked at the values of those in third sector (not-for-profit or charitable) organizations, which will include the majority of Christian agencies and churches.[83] They found there were eight which were especially important:

- Empowering people
- Making voices heard
- Being responsible
- Doing a good job
- Pursuing equality
- Transforming lives
- Finding fulfilment
- Generating public wealth

Although none of these are explicitly spiritual, much of the religious work done by churches and agencies would fall within several of these values. Their report indicates that these values inspire people to work and volunteer in the third sector, but that organizations can be deflected from following them by not focussing on them or allowing administrative demands to overshadow them.

A multi-faith Church of England primary school called Holy Trinity, in Buckinghamshire, contained Christian, Muslim, Hindu and Sikh children, as well as those with no faith. The Christian children went to the headteacher and said, 'We think one of our values should be 'What would Jesus do?" which is often abbreviated WWJD. The head teacher talked to the Muslims, who didn't mind as Jesus was one of their prophets. The Hindus talked about this unusual value at great length, but finally agreed as it was a Christian school. 'So it was agreed that WWJD should become one of the school's values, one of the critera by which everything that happens in that school should be evaluated.'[84] It was as if the children were looking back through a future door and seeing something not obvious to everyone else, which can be how HMM works.

Applying HMM

HMM can be applied to the church scene just as it can to any secular organization. The essence of it is to travel, as it were, into the future. To help people do that in vision building seminars, I use a number of scenarios. It is hard for people to think in radically different ways when they have been used to a given situation for perhaps many years. They know others in the organization or congregation are familiar with their stories and the way they do things. To try and get them to consider new alternatives is not easy. So HMM suggests that they move to a situation that is new for everybody. In this way they all have a level playing field. The professor's experience may count for no more than the thoughts of someone just out of school. Each has to imagine a different world. Some people's imaginations are better than others, but it does not follow that creative people will necessarily do best.

So what happens in these seminars? After a description of the process, a future scenario is described, such as pretending we are in the year 2040 when everyone goes blind when they are 30, or a plane crashed on top of your church, or there was a severe earthquake which caused everything over two stories to collapse, or a meteor crashed into the Isle of Man and the UK is experiencing severe floods everywhere.[85]

Those present are divided into groups of 6 to 8 people and asked to react to what they have heard. We find it best if the groups are asked two questions at intervals, the first being a neutral, non-Christian question (to get them used to the idea of being many years ahead), and then a specifically Christian question. Their answers are not written down, although to make the activity more lively, the groups are sometimes asked to vote which group gave the best answers. Each person in the winning group then gets a packet of sweets or something similar.

Subsequently, they are asked why they gave the answers they did, and these answers are written down on a flip chart so that everyone can see them. It is these answers which help to begin teasing out the values that were being applied in the future scene. This is where the assumption about values comes in, because *these future values are almost certainly the same ones* as drive them today.

Once the values have been listed and everyone has had the opportunity to contribute and indicate any that have been missed, they are asked to prioritize them. Each person chooses the three they think are most important and the three they think important but not most important. We then go through the values one by one asking those who felt them most important to put two hands up, and those who felt them partly important just one hand. Counting the votes in this way determines the values which the present audience feels are most important. It is worthwhile to help people reflect on the new list and to acknowledge that these are indeed the key values of the church or organization. There is an additional question which is usually worth asking at this juncture: 'What values will you not sacrifice in order to accomplish your vision?'

The second scenario is usually one much closer to the present period of time, say 10 or 15 years ahead. Its purpose is different. In a church context I usually suggest that a new minister has come to your church in 2015 and that your group is giving him or her induction information on what the church has achieved in the last five years. The aim now is not to determine the values but to try and uncover the implicit assumptions people are making on the changes they expect to have taken place over these next few years in their situation. These again are listed on a flip chart, and are again prioritized. We then have two lists – values deemed most important, changes most likely to have been made. Sometimes there is overlap between the two.

By this time people are usually 'hooked' and there is often an excited buzz of conversation over lunch. When we get back together we use the two lists created in the morning, starting with the top issues which emerged from the changes. Groups are asked to each come back with up to 3 practical suggestions which they feel should begin to happen immediately in the church or agency. Again there can well be overlap in their answers, which are again noted down.

BHAGs

Some of these suggestions are readily and easily applied, but sometimes a BHAG emerges. This is why this process is creative. I always tell the organizer, if asked to lead a vision building seminar in this way, that I cannot guess what the outcome will be in advance.

BHAG? This stands for **B**ig **H**airy **A**udacious **G**oal, and is usually pronounced 'Be-hag'! It is an American term. It is

> a powerful mechanism in an organization. More than a goal, a BHAG is a "take the mountain" kind of challenge. . . . A BHAG is clear and compelling and serves as a unifying focal point of effort. It also requires a high level of commitment, not to the leader, but to the goal. It is not a statement but must engage and capture people's spirit.[86]

When President John Kennedy announced in 1961 that he wanted to see a man on the moon by the end of the 1960s, it was a BHAG. It thrilled and excited many people across America. A BHAG connects with people immediately. It is concrete and invigorating. They are easily understandable, needing barely any explanation, if any.[87] As someone once said, 'Shoot for the moon. Even if you fail, you'll land among the stars.'

BHAGs are the real innovation. They allow you to get out of a rut, turn the rules of the game around and make considerable impact.[88] LandSecurities had an interesting series of adverts on 'Evolving Britain' in 2008. Their slogans were 'Making the library go to the kids if the kids won't go to the library' (putting the school library next to the front entrance of a school); 'Building a public park over 600 feet in the air' (putting some botanical gardens on top of 20 Fenchurch Street with a 360 degree panorama of London); and 'Making sure new shopping centres have shops you've never heard of' (reserving a street just for independent retailers in their redevelopment of the Princess Hay centre in Exeter). This is BHAG-type thinking, and all these examples have important implicit values.

Other stimuli for BHAG thinking are questions like 'What would you attempt to do if you knew you could not fail?' or 'What would you do if you'd just been raised from the dead?'[89]

Does it work?

The purpose of HMM is to help a church gain a vision, and to think strategically as to how that vision may be accomplished. It is based on values and creativity. Sometimes what emerges is a plethora of what might be described as mini-visions. When that happened in one church, the minister was delighted – 'You've given me my programme for the coming year or so.' On the other hand, sometimes a BHAG emerges – one church decided to build a new church hall in order to meet the needs of those on their estate in a real and practical way.

The values which emerge are often of three broad types, and frequently emerge in this order:

1 The need to *share* the resources of those in the church with those without access to such.

2 The need to *help* people in their social, physical or family circumstances. This is essentially the desire to work in, with and for the local community.

3 The desire to *provide* opportunities for people to hear the gospel, or learn about what the church believes.

What is different with HMM?

Horizon Mission Methodology does not work in the same way as the vision building method. Table 5.2 shows some of the differences.

Table 4.2: Different ways of vision formation

VISION BUILDING	HORIZON MISSION METHODOLOGY
Developed by management consultants	Developed by NASA scientists
Moves from past to near future	Moves from distant future to near future
Invariably linear	Rarely linear
Logical, progressive	Intuitive, creative
Focuses on statements	Focuses on values
Strategic planning a part of the process	Strategic planning a separate process
Few BHAGs	More BHAGs

Some years ago, the Chair of one of the larger Evangelical mission agencies asked Christian Research to help with a Vision Building Day. At that time we did not know of HMM so used the traditional method. A year or so later a church in Southampton asked us to run a Vision Building Day for them, and in discussion with the pastor, we used HMM. Imagine my surprise when the Chair of the agency turned out to be one of the deacons of the church.

As he personally experienced both methods I asked him his reactions. The traditional Vision Building Day, he said, helps to sharpen thinking and praying. It can be used to challenge others as it focuses on specific goals. It allows extrapolation and he felt it challenges leaders to return to core values. Horizon Mission Methodology, on the other hand, threw up many interesting concepts and possibilities. He felt it allows ideas from more people to be heard, and thus encourages a more inclusive ministry. He thought thinking future would inspire some to dynamic involvement, but proposed that it was easier for churches to change direction than agencies, and that therefore HMM was perhaps more useful for churches.

This was a helpful comparison. It shows the specific nature of vision building which is readily appreciated, but also shows that HMM is wide-ranging across both ideas and people – and it offers greater opportunities for involvement.

Looking in a different direction

Trying to look to the future by looking backwards may seem an odd phenomenon. I enjoy taking holidays in Scotland where I am awed by the majestic landscape. Going along some of the minor roads, you come across isolated houses or cottages facing magnificent panoramas. Sometimes, however, you find such houses facing tangentially to the major view, as if they were built facing the wrong direction. There may be good reasons for that, such as the prevailing winds, but it means that the owners don't naturally see the view ahead when in their front room.

Perhaps the wild scenery is already so much in their soul that they don't need to repeatedly look at it. The vision is so embedded within them that they can look in other directions for all the subsidiary things that are part of everyday life, perhaps keeping an eye on their cattle. HMM can be a sufficiently robust process to enable such a sure vision to be formed that you can look at other facets of the process with confidence. 'When God gives you a vision, he doesn't usually give you a map, but he does give you a compass-bearing.'[90]

CAN THESE DRY BONES LIVE?

This is a *searching* question. The prophet Ezekiel was called to take a step of faith. His career had not turned out as expected. He was a man who loved detail, and would date the key events in his life so precisely that two and a half millennia later we can know them exactly.

He was born in the country of Judah in 623 BC, and grew up while good King Josiah was on the throne. Josiah died in 609 BC in the needless battle of Megiddo with Pharaoh Neco, when Ezekiel was 14 (2 Kgs 23:29). Josiah had made a number of religious reforms and had re-introduced the keeping of the Passover.

Ezekiel was trained as a priest but, when undergoing this training in his teenage years, would have seen the developing problems of governance in a small country when Josiah's successor, Jehoahaz, was replaced after just 3 months by Jehoiakim, both of whom had totally different values from Josiah. Jehoiakim reigned only till 598 BC, when Ezekiel was 25. That year his world was turned upside down. The Babylonian emperor Nabopolassar sent his son King Nebuchadnezzar to invade Judah in 598 BC. He captured Jerusalem and took several thousand Jews into exile to his capital city nearly 700 miles away. As a working minister, Ezekiel was one of those wrenched from his homeland to a foreign country from which he would never return.

After five years in a totally different culture, surrounded by a national religious environment which was abhorrent to him, but presumably still able to serve the people as best he could, Ezekiel received a divine message. On 31 July 593 BC the Lord gave him a vision of his transcendency, sovereignty and judgement. 'When I saw it, I fell on my face, and I heard the voice of someone speaking' (Ezek. 1:28).

Ezekiel was called to be a prophet, a new vocation which he performed admirably. He had a difficult assignment – to convince the exiles that God's judgement really had come, and they would not be going back to their homes, fields and relatives. They would die in Babylon. In 586 BC, when Ezekiel was 37, the blow finally came. Nebuchadnezzar had invaded the troublesome country of Judah, which had refused to pay him taxes – again. This time the walls were broken down, the unimaginable happened with the Temple being smashed to pieces, all the king's children were slain followed by the luckless, but deliberately defiant, King Zedekiah having both his eyes put out.

Ezekiel's job changed overnight. From being a messenger of gloom (judgement was coming; contrary to popular thinking, Jerusalem was not inviolable) he had to become a herald of hope (God would not leave the Jews in Babylon forever). Ezekiel preached, acted, prophesied. God gave him visions to help him understand the issues, finally giving him a wonderful vision of the new Jerusalem, on New Year's Day 573 BC, when Ezekiel was 50. Ezekiel, true to his innate desire for accuracy, spelled it all out complete with measurements. But a new Jerusalem had to be inhabited by a renewed people, and that was the subject of yet another vision.

In that vision, Ezekiel was placed in the middle of a valley which was full of human bones. He noted there were a great many of them, and that they were very dry (Ezek. 37:2). God asked him a question, 'Can these dry bones live?' Ezekiel, knowing something of God's power and positive purposes for his people, in effect said, 'Yes, Lord, you know.' God then told him to prophesy to the bones – what, preach to dead objects? But, like other servants of God, Ezekiel was obedient and did so. It was only as he spoke, however, that the bones began coming together, forming themselves once again into human beings and after a further specific prophecy, that breath came into them, and they stood on their feet, alive – a restored people fit for the work of God! As Derek Hills pointed out in a sermon on Ezekiel 37, two things were needed for this revival: the word of the Lord – no place is so hopeless that the word of God can't change it – and the breath of God – bringing the power for change (Tonbridge Baptist Church, Jan. 2008).

Ezekiel may have known the Lord God quite well, but he still had to go ahead and speak to inanimate things, believing (hoping) that something would happen. That is precisely what we have to do with our vision. God puts us in a certain location, helps us to see everything that's all around, gives us a vision of how it could be, and then, in the absence of anything physical, tells us to go ahead. The process is all about faith, and it's what Christianity is all about.

So how can we go forward when we believe we know what should be done but nothing has yet changed? This chapter looks at some of the obstacles for moving ahead, and the practical ways of overcoming them.

The invisible

Ezekiel didn't know what God was going to do. The bones might have all jumped up together in one fell swoop. They didn't – it was a gradual process. Ezekiel started doing what he was bidden, and, invisibly, some of the key forces for change began to do their work. That is frequently the case for us.

Actually, the invisible is crucially important. It is what some call 'under the radar', happening but not being seen to happen. General Sir Richard Dannatt, former Chief of the General Staff, gave a wonderful example in a lecture of the 'invisible' from the 1994 Bosnian campaign in which the British Army was asked to disarm the two warring sides.[91] The visible part of this operation was the nightly pictures shown on the news back home of the two sides handing over weapons to be neutralized. However, the military leaders felt this disarming of the warring parties would probably not be sufficient to bring lasting peace.

So the general in charge, General Sir Michael Rose, decided to persuade the Bosnian people that it was better to take the negotiated peace settlement offered through the United Nations, and thus live in peace, rather than continue fighting each other for their varying objectives.[92] In order to achieve this, the general and other senior members of the Army high command went and visited individual villages, talking with the local people and their leaders directly. It took a long time to talk through the options but eventually the invisible hope for peace proved stronger than the visible fighting, and the general and his colleagues won the day.

Another way of expressing this is asking the question: 'How could you add to what you're doing to make it more successful?' For example, a church has a new youth worker arriving in September. The church wants that person to work with the local schools as well as helping the young people's work in the church. The minister of the church, who has probably already met the head teachers of some of the local schools, could in, say, June or July, visit these head teachers for a chat and mention that the new school worker will be available to help with assemblies or RS lessons. This is laying a strategic foundation for others to build on, analogous to Paul's comment 'I planted, Apollos watered, but God gave the growth' (1 Cor. 3:6). It is doing the invisible.

The second vision

If a church is to grow, it is most likely to do so after a minister has been there for between 7 and 9 years,[93] with the next best length being 10 to 13 years. That is why many ministers feel what is sometimes called 'the 10-year itch'. However, some ministers stay on much longer than that and do so with acclaim. Others, on the other hand, move too soon, and see all their good work dissipate.

We worked with one church where a leader with lots of vision had successfully built a growing and thriving church. However, as he neared retirement, he lost some of his earlier energy and enthusiasm, and much of what he had gained was lost.

'I've been in my present church for 11 and a half years,' said a minister at one of our *Shaping the Future* seminars. 'Should I move on?' I replied, 'No, not if you have the courage to rethink your present strategy and formulate a new vision for the next 5 or so years.'

Somebody else asked, 'How can I best prepare to take over from my predecessor when he leaves the church in 2 years' time?' The answer is similar – not by continuing with his vision, but finding your own, or a new vision for the church, even though that may build on his.

How can this best be done? Not easily, but it is sometimes helpful to think through answers to questions like

1 What do you observe to be the key problems in your ministry? In the church in general? In your organization?

2 If you could change one thing about your present position, what would it be and why? (In other words, localize the problem as well as observing it in general terms: the answers may not be the same.)

3 What is the biggest hindrance you currently face with respect to evangelizing your local community? (This is a church question; if you are an agency, substitute whatever is your key task.) What could you do to remove or at least reduce its impact?

4 If resources were not a hindrance, what innovative feature would you bring in over the next 6 months?

This latter question is especially important as the thinking in it begins the process of strategy and, with that, the opportunity for vision. The answers to the questions need to be discussed with others, in your family, your church or your organization. Part of the task is to try and envision them to think beyond the obvious – not just to go faster down the existing track, but to branch out on a new track, or tack, altogether.

There is a fifth question to add to the above, a much harder question to consider. I had the privilege of talking to one of the Kenyan bishops who, along with many others, had decided not to attend the 2008 Lambeth Conference. His views and those of some of the American Bishops on homosexuality were very different. His incisive comment was, 'If we feel they are wrong, what mistakes did we make along the way to cause that?' He agreed that sometimes we need to look backwards in order to focus forward more clearly. 'Anyone wishing to see what is to be,' said Machiavelli, 'must consider what has been.'[94]

No confidence in the deanery

The Anglican Hallam Deanery in High Wycombe had a problem – they had been asked to consider how the deanery might be led if the number of incumbents was gradually reduced from 16 to just 11 in a decade's time.[95] Should some churches close, or merge? Should greater collaboration take place with non-Anglican churches? Should non-Anglican ministers be employed instead? How could they make greater use of volunteers? All these are valid questions. However, it is important in such situations not to find a suitable solution which is based on the gifting of the current clergy or laity. Those involved need to think more widely – as if they were in a helicopter looking down on the situation – getting a bigger, broader overview of what is needed.

They decided it would be appropriate to have a Vision Building Day. The large majority of the churches attending decided their key problem was lack of confidence in the gospel. If there was more confidence, there should be more witnessing. If more witnessing, there should be more people coming to faith. If more conversions, the churches should begin to grow, not decline. With growth and greater resources, various alternative solutions to fewer clergy could be considered. The conclusion of the day was to ask the Area Dean for training in how to grow in confidence. That is 'helicopter' (or BHAG) thinking.

Collaboration of different interests

The URC Church at Bromley-by-Bow (www.bbbc.org.uk) was close to a small park in a difficult, run-down area of London which was 65% Muslim. Their congregation in the 1990s was tiny. Getting a first vision, let alone a second, was not easy. However, the leadership talked with others in the area who did not want the church to close. Instead, a long-term agreement was made between the local authority and a medical team (who were allowed to build a medical centre in the park alongside the church). The inside of the church was totally re-ordered around a central diamond with 'sails' above and a children's play area on the circumference, to allow for community use.

Ten years later, the local park has been adapted (with a tea shop), and the complex contains a café, a housing advice centre, the medical centre, a roof garden (to grow vegetables used in the café), a sculpture shop and adult training classes in the arts, including glass and woodwork. A single architect designed it all. While the church gets only up to 20 on a Sunday, over 1,000 use the building during the week.

They have achieved their vision of not closing: now for the vision to grow!

Renewing the transport dream

How could anyone get a second vision for St Pancras? It had been built as a railway station in 1868 for receiving coal transported from the Midlands to London. The Eurostar headquarters had been situated several miles away over a new concourse at Waterloo International. Richard Brown became the CEO a few years ago and initiated a plan to stimulate visionary thinking. Eurostar had been knocked over the years and performance had deteriorated. Richard brought in fresh people, 'the best in their field', took many hours to convince the upper echelons of the company, and 'gambled pretty heavily on the opening of High Speed 1 to turn everything round'. The idea that St Pancras could be used for European departures took some while to be accepted (not least because of the huge cost). A publicity drive was launched and it worked. In 2006 Eurostar carried nearly 8 million passengers, a 30% rise in two years, bringing in more than £500 million, an 11% rise over the previous year, and a stunningly restored Victorian gothic St Pancras opened as Eurostar's new headquarters and London terminal in the presence of the Queen.[96]

Larger churches

Second (or third or fourth) visions do not come quickly or easily, but they come from looking at what still needs to be done, and how you, or your church or organization, can contribute to it. Often they need, like human beings, two parents – one for the imaginative ideas and the other for the dedicated follow-through. The first may find it hard to take the necessary risks, but the second is the detailed achiever with the courage to make it happen. Occasionally, these roles combine in one person, but such are rare.[97]

We will look at the crucial importance of larger churches in chapter 6, but many of them are prime examples of second visions, and working in partnership. A 2008 survey showed that almost half are appointing a 'Chief of Staff', 'Director of Operations', or a person with some such title, to work alongside the senior minister. Simply, the senior minister is responsible for the spiritual side of the work, the Director of Operations for everything else, such as

- Staff appointments and evaluations.
- Team formulation and building.
- Handling people's expectations.
- Building maintenance, and insurance.
- Risk strategy.
- Organizational structure.
- Finance.
- Welcoming and introductory procedures.
- Thinking about the future (second and subsequent visions and succession problems).

Of course, this is not a solo performance, but such a person is, in effect, the manager responsible for key staff looking after the day-to-day detail in these various areas. A major part of the role is relational, making sure the team works well together. That necessitates regular team meetings (with prepared agendas in advance), keeping the vision under control (asking team leaders how they are working towards it), and encouraging a sense of openness, and consequently, unity. They help to avoid the danger of the church or organization operating in a number of isolated, independent and self-contained units.

Leadership training

One might expect that pastors would have some of the gifting seen in such 'Directors of Operation'. What happens if churches do not wish to have, or cannot afford, or cannot find, a Director of Operations? This leads to a different question, on the training of those for leadership. It is interesting that one large church, Holy Trinity Brompton, has begun its own training institution, St Mellitus College. A close observer of the international theological training scene, Dr Manfred Kohl, urges that

> theological education must give more attention to churches and their needs; be more mission oriented; put greater effort into spiritual formation as part of ministry skills; focus on training outcomes, on the effectiveness of graduates in ministry; rediscover the value in practical mentorship; address the needs of the laity and must be a regular renewal program, new wine as well as new wine skins.[98]

HTB is not the only ones involved in radical training. The Arrow Programme, developed by American evangelist Leighton Ford, is pursued enthusiastically in the UK by CPAS under the leadership of James Lawrence[99] (whose book *Growing Leaders* – see bibliography – sums up much of Arrow's teaching).

The Australian Peter Kaldor found people typically feel poorly equipped for the realities of church leadership. The National Church Life Survey found that 44% of ministers say it is much more challenging than expected, and 30% say they are out of their depth.[100]

Invisible leadership

I guess when Ezekiel had finished prophesying and the army of revived Israelite bones was all around him, they didn't rush to thank him for their resurrection. The outcome of what he had done was obvious but what he had done to get that far was not.

Janet Cohen

In 1994, Janet Cohen was married with three children, two of whom were still at home. She was a governor of the BBC, and on the boards of the Sheffield Development Corporation and Yorkshire Building Society. She was in a senior position at Charterhouse Bank, for which she worked 3 days a week. In the years 1988 to1994 she wrote five novels, four of them crime stories, of which one won a Crime Writers' Association award. 'I started,' she said, 'because I heard Phyllis [P.D.] James on the radio saying that she had thought she would start writing when her life calmed down a bit, and then one day she realized that her life was never going to calm down.' So how does Cohen do all that? 'I owe it to my mother-in-law,' she said, 'who taught me that *you can shift the world if you do it half an hour at a time*. I write for a couple of hours a day: no fussing, no waiting for creative inspiration. Not a lot happens until I sit down behind a desk.' [italics mine][101] Invisible commitment?

Sonia Gandhi

Beautiful Sonia Maino was born in Italy but married Rajiv Gandhi – who was from one of the most influential families in India. Her husband served briefly as prime minister of India in the 1980s but was assassinated in 1991. Sonia Gandhi remained in India with her two children, but after many requests, entered the turbulent world of Indian politics a few years ago. Many begged her to become prime minister, but, to the astonishment of people around the world she turned it down. She remains one of the people, and leaves the power to others. This is a remarkable story at many levels.

> That of the Italian who became the most powerful figure in a land of a billion Indians? That of the reluctant politician who led her party to power? That of the parliamentary leader who rejected the highest office in her adopted land, one she had earned by her hard work and political courage? That of the woman of principle who demonstrated that one could stand for the right values even in a profession corroded by cynicism and cant? That of the novice in politics who became a master of the art, trusted her own instincts and discovered she could be right more often than her jaded rivals could ever have imagined? The story of Sonia Gandhi must be all of these stories, and more.[102]

Invisible strategy?

Ahmed Saad

Ahmed Saad became a Muslim imam earlier this decade, but he was born into a family of scholars, all of whom, from his great-grandfather downwards, had become imams. He had learnt the Koran by heart by the time he was 10. As an imam, he says

> I have to be sociable and a good speaker. An imam is a leader in the community. I have to help people solve all types of problems: psychological, family and financial. I lead five daily prayers and run courses in Islamic education, leadership and team-building. We're establishing a gym at the mosque. When I arrived here in 2007, there were about 50 people coming. Now on Fridays we get 1,000 people, sometimes 2,500. People just need to feel secure. It doesn't give much time for my family, but it's lively and every day I've got something new. Sometimes I put my name in Google to see people's feedback on me. It touches my heart when I read something good.[103]

Invisible self-esteem?

Information Technology

Ezekiel didn't have access to the technology God used to raise his people's bones and lived in a primitive society: unlike today where we use technology undreamed of even 10 years ago.

Web 2.0, blogs, wikis and YouTube are words in use as I write, but which will be out-of-date in probably just 3 years' time. Books can now be downloaded on mobile phone-sized devices.

Alison Morgan puts her finger on the point.

> I have found it fascinating to feel the challenge of the internet to my habitual ways of thinking. It is, I find, impossible to use it in any way which is compatible with the old linear patterns of rational thought. Every time I follow a link, a new screenful of information bursts into my mind. These links do not operate in straight lines but in sideways jumps, and I experience a constant interruption to my train of thought, and the increasing stress of trying to remember where I came from so that I can get back there.[104]

It is not just that IT is booming, growing and changing at an incredible pace, but that its very structure affects the way we see things. I once suggested to an audience of people mostly in their 20s at a *Reaching and Keeping Tweenagers* seminar that I thought the Bible took a linear view of history, and nearly caused a mass walk-out because so many disagreed with me. Part of the challenge for leadership today is not just how to be relevant, but how to *think* relevantly.

The whole process of management is changing also. Plummeting communication costs and globalization are opening up a horde of competitors, including church-based sites like St Pixels. Managing IT systems is one challenge, but the much greater one is dealing with the impact of so many thinking in contrasting ways. And it is not just in our thinking – the web is altering the ways in which we relate to and collaborate or socialize with each other.[105] Humanity is on the move! It is the *flow* of knowledge that is important, not just having *banks* of knowledge: 'ensure that your organization . . . is supporting, not constraining, the sharing of knowledge.'[106] Can these dry screens live? Michael Moynagh, of Fresh Expressions, would argue that side-to-side contact, peer-level sharing, is precisely what helps to make a good Fresh Expressions experiment, but acknowledges that it needs a strategy to make it a success.[107]

This will mean standing up for the truth when we see it being twisted, torn and shredded on the web.[108] 'Courage,' said Nelson Mandela, 'is not the absence of fear – it's inspiring others to move beyond it.'[109]

Praying into the future

The question 'Can these dry bones live?' echoes down the centuries. It brings us to the urgent and important need to pray, and to pray for the future.

Families

Hudson Taylor began the China Inland Mission in 1865. He was one of several missionaries to that great country a century and a half ago. Hudson married Maria and they had children. Hudson and Maria prayed for their family as probably all Christian parents do. But they didn't just pray for their children – they prayed for the other Christian families bringing up children of about the age of theirs whom their children would meet one day and marry. And after praying for their potential sons- and daughters-in-law they prayed for the children these couples would have – that is, their grandchildren. They went further and prayed similarly for the partners their grandchildren would meet and for their children also, Hudson and Maria's great-grandchildren. They prayed into the future down to the third and fourth generation. In 1965 the society changed its name to the Overseas Missionary Fellowship (or OMF International as it is known today). The seventh General Director, James Taylor, who was General Director in the 1980s, was one of Hudson Taylor's great-grandchildren, prayed for by the founder himself 100 or so years before.

James Dobson, who has done so much for families during his lifetime, says that his great-grandfather asked the Lord to give him all in his family down to the fourth generation. James, in that fourth generation, can testify that all his direct relatives are Christians.

Do we pray for our children? Our grandchildren? Our great-grandchildren? Even our great-great-grandchildren? Or our nieces and nephews or cousin's children if we are not married? Let your mind stretch into the future as you pray. What might God have in store for your family? Why not pray for the husbands your daughters will marry or for the wives your sons will marry? Somewhere someone else is bringing them up even now.

Whom will your children meet? Why not pray for their friends and the friendships that will form from them? What influence will each have on the other, and will it be for good or bad? What will your children, your grandchildren, hear, read, watch on TV, see on the web or DVD? How will their Christian consciousness be increased? What might cause it to be deadened? How best to pray?

Grandparents

There are some 800,000 churchgoing grandparents.[110] Is there a place for bringing them together to pray for their children and grandchildren? In some churches where there are mostly older people, they club together to list all their grandchildren's birthdays, and grand-nieces and grand-nephews of those who had no grandchildren. Then, each week, the leader prays for those whose birthday would be that week. Some such churches begin to grow as a consequence, as families moving into their village realized when they attended that children were welcomed and valued.

Churches

It is also possible to pray for the future churches in our land, and their leaders, some of whom are undergoing training at this very moment, and some of whom have yet to be born. What will influence them as they grow up? Who will hear the call to serve? Will that service just be for the church in the UK or for the church across the world? Mission workers are likely to get fewer in number in the days ahead.[111] We should we praying for more: 'Ask the Lord of the harvest to send out laborers into his harvest' (Matt. 9:38).

When Paul was travelling across the known world, his strategy was to start city churches so that in turn they could evangelize the hinterland. In so doing, he was using his gifts as an apostle and church planter. What gifts do the people in your church have? How can the doctor be helped to live out her faith among the people on her ward? How should we pray for the overworked manager in his office? In what ways can the retired teacher be encouraged to share her faith?

Some years ago a group of graduates who met regularly in Bromley, Kent did a 'gift evaluation' of themselves and found they had many with the gift of teaching. They then asked themselves how could they collectively use that gift? God will have given diverse gifts to those in your congregation: how best can these be prayed through and used for his service?

Agencies or organizations

Similar thinking helps people to pray for their organization or business. Not every Christian organization is intended to last for ever. As you pray for the future of your work, might the Lord be saying it should close or merge with another organization, now or in a few years' time? If your agency is a Christian one, does it have regular devotions? Do meetings start with prayer? In one Christian group every agenda always had an opening and closing item – prayer – whatever else was on the agenda. In at least one town known to me, the town council starts its meetings with prayer led by its chaplain.

Praying for the future often means thinking future, and thinking carefully. Some agencies work through associates in other countries. *Operation World* is an excellent guide for those wishing to pray for the different countries around our globe. Working through such a book gives a person a much better idea of the Christian situation worldwide.

If your organization or business has a clear vision, then praying for the future is praying to help that vision become reality. Ezekiel's visions were to give hope and encouragement to people living in difficult circumstances in Babylon. Maybe the visions of those we work for can likewise give us hope as we pray for their fulfilment and see situations improve as a consequence.

Can these dry bones live?

Ezekiel's reply 'O Lord GOD, you know,' (37:3) may have expressed his own inadequacy but also his deep conviction in the sovereign knowledge and power of his God. This is probably of closer application to where we are, that is, a vision of doubling our congregation in 5 years' time may seem impossible, but the way forward is to trust in the almighty power of God to unfold and use the means by which it can be achieved.

In this chapter we have looked at the importance of trusting God in faith as Ezekiel did, thinking about the invisible actions we can take to support our visible actions, methods of getting a second vision, the strategic value of larger churches, the ways in which effective leadership may be totally unseen, the need to embrace Information Technology but noting that it can distort the way we think, and, not least, the huge benefit of praying into the future for our families and workplaces. So, why wait?

REFLECTION: WHY WAIT?

During the Second World War, an American bomber with seven crewmen took off from its base in North Africa to bomb Naples in Italy. Its job accomplished, it headed home, but it never arrived. For many years the fate of the *Lady Be Good* was a mystery, and it was thought that it had run out of fuel and crashed in the Mediterranean. It was found almost 20 years later ditched in the Sahara desert, 442 miles past its destination.

It had plenty of fuel, but that night an unusually strong tail wind caused the bomber to reach the North African coast well ahead of schedule. Their flight instruments indicated they had flown far enough, but the crew couldn't believe it, assuming you could not fly so far in so short a time. Believing the enemy had somehow jammed their instruments, or that they were malfunctioning, the officer in charge decided to continue. The decision cost him and his crew their lives.[112]

They had the right information, but chose not to act on it. Many of us will know the story of the boy walking along the seashore where thousands of starfish had been washed up. As he walked along, he picked up a starfish and threw it back into the sea. 'You'll never rescue all those starfish,' his companion said, 'there are far too many.' 'True,' said the boy, as he picked another up, 'but it makes all the difference for this one.' He had the right information, was not overwhelmed by it, and did what he could.

As the moon slid over the sun in a total eclipse, a picture was taken showing the corona of the sun. Could the

146

church ever be eclipsed like the sun was at that moment? No, because Jesus is building his church and the gates of hell will not prevail against it (Matt. 16:18). Although the Scriptures bid us wait on the Lord for guidance, waiting does not necessarily exclude prayerful action.

This book has looked at five questions of God:

Chapters 1&6	Where are you?	Our place in the big picture
Chapter 2	What is that in your hand?	Understanding ourselves
Chapter 3	What are you doing here?	Sorting out priorities
Chapter 4	What do you see?	Clarifying our vision
Chapter 5	Can these dry bones live?	Working with the invisible

These are five issues that have often been raised by Christian leaders of churches or by agencies, organizations or businesses in terms of their leadership. They have plenty of other questions, but these seem to be the main ones, though they may not be phrased exactly as in this book. If some of these are your questions also, now is the time to take the key decision to do something, to begin taking strategic actions to change or enhance your life's work.

The sub-title of this book is 'Vision, Strategy and Growth'. All three words are important, and need to be taken in this order.

Vision: What will you become?

This is the element which looks to the future. What is it that you want to become? Where are you going? Or, if that is too vague, what will you have become in 10 years' time? (The number 10 is completely variable, but the period should probably be for at least 3 years ahead.)

One of Solomon's proverbs is unambiguous – 'Where there is no vision the people perish' (Prov. 29:18, KJV). The way different translations of the Bible handle this verse is illuminating.

'People break loose without a guiding hand'. (Moffatt)

'Where there is no vision, the people get out of hand'. (Jerusalem)

'Where there is no revelation, the people cast off restraint'. (RAV & NIV)

'Where there is no prophecy, the people cast off restraint'. (NRSV)

'Where there is no one in authority, the people break loose'. (NEB)

'A nation without God's guidance is a nation without order'. (GNB)

'When people do not accept divine guidance, they run wild'. (New Living Bible)

'Without guidance from God law and order disappear'. (CEV)

'When there is no prophetic vision, the people unravel'. (literal translation[113]).

Two of the alternative words used for vision in these translations, revelation and prophecy, are used elsewhere in the Scriptures to translate the same Hebrew word. The need for help, clear leadership and firm understanding comes through. Without vision, however, it is not only the people who will perish. Without vision society perishes. Without vision, the church perishes. Without vision, the parachurch agency perishes. Without vision, you and I perish. Vision is not an optional extra, it is essential. As blind and deaf Helen Keller once said, 'There is only one thing worse than being blind . . . being able to see, but having no vision.'

> The core of leadership is vision. Vision is seeing the potential purpose hidden in the chaos of the moment, but which could bring to birth new possibilities for a person, a company or a nation.[114]

Vision is tracing the divine story unfolding in the past, the present and the future. Chaotic moments trouble most of us at some time or other. Nevertheless, what do you see as you look through your particular chaos?

Strategy: what are you planning?

On his way through the (presumably) moonlit streets of Jerusalem, after the Last Supper, after Judas has left to go to the religious leaders, Jesus is talking with his disciples. They are walking towards Gethsemane. The conversation is familiar to us, for it's when Peter declares that while everyone else may desert Jesus, he never will, and Jesus tells him that before the cock crows that night, he will deny him three times (Matt. 26:33,34).

Jesus knew he was walking towards Gethsemane, where anguish, betrayal, arrest, false trial, scourging, mocking, condemnation, crucifixion and resurrection all awaited him, and all, except the last, in the next 12 hours. In that conversation with his companions, however, Jesus also says, 'But after I am raised up, I will go ahead of you to Galilee'.

There are 40 days between the resurrection of Jesus and his ascension into heaven. Exactly when they all met up for breakfast one morning on the shores of Lake Galilee, where Jesus and Peter had another intimate conversation, we don't know (John 21:15–19). Suppose it was roughly half way through those 40 days. Then, in effect, what Jesus said to the apostles en route for Gethsemane was, 'Boys, I'll see you by the Lake in three weeks time.' *That* is strategic thinking. Jesus was already sharing how he would use those precious final 40 days on earth in order to fulfil his objective of building a church which would resist the gates of hell. After the resurrection, the angel, too, reinforced Jesus' promise, 'He has been raised . . . he is going ahead of you to Galilee' (Mark 16:6).

Jesus maintained 'emotional objectivity whilst in the midst of an emotional system that [was] in turmoil – and at the same time actively relate[d] to the key people in the system.'[115] Jesus calls us to follow him and promises that he will go before.

Growth: what is about to happen?

> Faith is a matter of the heart, not head. Our heart has to be ahead of our head.[116]

While that is undoubtedly true, it is also important that we think aright too. Interpreting 'Be careful how you think; your life is shaped by your thoughts' (Prov. 4:23, GNB), one preacher made these 6 observations.

- My interpretation influences my situation.

- My impressions influence my depression.

- My beliefs influence my behaviour.

- My self-talk influences my self-esteem.

- My attitudes influence my ability.

- My imaginations influence my aspirations.[117]

As one human resources expert put it: 'Think "plumbing" as well as "grand plan", and remember every house starts with one brick.'[118] While the overall vision is crucial, it is actually built up bit by bit. It may be good to say that the UK has 6 million church members, which it has, but that number is built up by adding together all the members in the 275 individual denominations.

Growth requires teamwork too; the greatest success stories are not solo efforts. I once saw this summarized as

Coming together is a beginning

Keeping together is progress

Working together is success.

Courage and humility

One part of the book *The Mind Gym* looks at the issue of success and humility and suggests the following:

Open up. Get the most out of your team by welcoming their views. Appreciate everyone's contributions and you'll create more innovative solutions together.

Go for gold, not glory. Author Jim Collins compared the performance of high-profile CEOs with those who stay out of the limelight, and found that it is results, not status, that counts. Focus on your role, not your profile.

Don't tell, show. You don't have to be full of charisma, but simply demonstrate the high standards you expect. Inspiring behaviour can be more powerful than an inspiring speech.

Let others shine. Deflect discussions about yourself by praising the contributions of others. Lou Gerstner, who stopped IBM from crumbling in the 1990s, illustrates this: 'Change came to IBM in large part due to the pride and energy of the employees themselves. ... My role was to kick-start the process.'

Have faith. Coleman Mocker turned Gillette around, and retained remarkable balance in his work and home life – even during the darkest times of takeover crisis. His secret? Trusting the team that he'd assembled. Cultivate a team of experts and they'll build greatness, even when you're not there.[119]

Humility is not something one achieves; it is the result of other pursuits. It grows through walking in the shadow of the Master. 'A humble man,' said Isaak of Syria, 'is never hurried, hasty or perturbed, but at all times remains calm. Nothing can ever surprise, disturb, or dismay him, for he suffers neither fear nor change in tribulations, neither surprise nor elation in enjoyment. All his joy and gladness are in what is pleasing to the Lord.'[120] Here is a man who is talking about *pace* as a requirement for humility – humble people don't hurry, they have the patience to wait. At the same time, however, they are not idle – they keep going, and recognition can come later. It is like those of whom Indira Gandhi spoke, 'There are two kinds of people, those who do the work and those who take the credit. Try to be in the first group; there is less competition there.'[121]

The words of the soldier Byrthwold, who was about to die in the battle at Maldon in 961, recorded in the Old English poem, *Beowulf*, are worth repeating

Mind must be stronger,

Heart must be bolder,

Courage must be greater,

As our power grows less.

Go for it!

If you only look at what is, you might never attain what could be. There was a striking advert once, in which a teenage girl writes on a blackboard

SAY NO TO NO.

Isn't it time someone got negative about negativity?

Yes, it is . . .

What does it take to turn no into yes?

Curiosity. An open mind. A willingness to take risks.

And, when the problem seems most insoluble, when the challenge is hardest, when everyone else is shaking their heads, to say: Let's go.

We need to do just that – take faith and courage in both hands and say to God, 'Let's go!'

SECTION 2
THE CONTEXT

6

WHERE WE ARE

T S Eliot once asked where, in all our information, is knowledge and where, in all our knowledge, is wisdom?[122]

Looking at where we are should be balanced by looking at where others are as well, so here we look at the external context bypassed in chapter 1. This allows us to compare ourselves with wider trends; in some comparisons your church or organization will be stronger than others, and in some weaker. Both lead to strategic questions.

- If you are stronger than someone else, how can you build on that strength while you still have it? Opportunities do not last for ever.

- If you are not as strong as you would like to be in a certain sector, why is that? Can you identify the real reasons as well as the superficial reasons? The 'real reasons' are likely to be cultural, longer-term, deeper and perhaps more intimate or spiritual.

One book looking at future issues is *Going Global* by Moynagh and Worsley.[123] They identify 8 key global issues – the global economy, migration, communication, governance, business success, the 'war on terror' and crime, change and global energy. These factors correlate together and form the 'wider world' context.

Between the individual church or agency and the wider world sits another factor – what is happening to the wider church. In drawing an answer to the question, 'Where are you?' part of the colouring will be what is sometimes called 'the big picture'. This chapter looks at seven features which impact the Christian scene in the UK and further afield.

1) Decline: living in injury time

This fascinating phrase is used by Philip Jenkins, 'one of America's best scholars of religion' (according to *The Economist*[124]) when he was repeating a sermon heard from Malawi. 'We are now living in injury time, like in a football match,' he had said, emphasizing the temporary nature of life.[125] It can, however, be applied precisely to the British situation in which the number of people attending church is declining rapidly.

The number of adults and children attending a church in England on an average Sunday:

1979	5.4 million people	12% of the population
1989	4.7 million people	10%
1998	3.7 million people	7.5%
2005	3.2 million people	6.3%.[126]

The rate of decline in these figures is slowing. In the 9 years 1989 to 1998, the drop was 1 million people, but between 1998 and 2005, a 7 year period, it was only 0.5 million. If it had been continuing to decline at the previous rate, the number in 2005 would have been about 2.9 million people. It was because of this hiccup in the rate of decline that the book giving the commentary on the figures is called *Pulling out of the Nosedive*. What caused the extra quarter of a million people to be in church? Largely the black churches, whose importance we will look at shortly.

Rates of change are different for each country

The above figures for England are based on church censuses which took place in the years shown. In Scotland there were censuses in 1984, 1994 and 2002, and in Wales in 1982 and 1995. There has never been one in Northern Ireland. If all the results are put together and then adjusted to every five years, then the figures for church attendance in Great Britain are:

Table 6.1: Churchgoers on an Average Sunday in Great Britain, 1980-2005

YEAR	ENGLAND		WALES		SCOTLAND		GREAT BRITAIN	
	Number	% of pop	Number	% of pop	Number	% of pop	Number	% of pop
1980	5,415,000	11.6	423,000	15.0	912,000	17.6	6,750,000	12.3
1985	4,965,000	10.5	366,000	13.0	834,000	16.3	6,165,000	11.1
1990	4,514,000	9.4	310,000	10.7	751,000	14.7	5,575,000	9.9
1995	4,063,000	8.3	253,000	8.6	677,000	13.2	4,993,000	8.8
2000	3,613,000	7.3	224,000	7.6	602,000	12.0	4,439,000	7.7
2005	3,166,000	6.3	200,000	6.7	511,000	10.0	3,877,000	6.6

The table shows that Welsh church attendance is declining fastest, dropping at an average rate of –3.0% per annum over these 25 years, followed by the Scottish at –2.3%, with England falling at –2.1%, less because of black church attendance again. Had the 2005 figure been 2.95 million, the rate of decline since 1980 would have been –2.4%. In these 25 years, 1980 to 2005, church attendance has effectively halved in Great Britain.

Future prognosis is not good (humanly speaking)

If we extend the figures of Table 6.1 for 25 years ahead, we get the results shown in Table 6.2:

Table 6.2: Churchgoers on an Average Sunday in Great Britain, 2005–2030

YEAR	ENGLAND Number	% of pop	WALES Number	% of pop	SCOTLAND Number	% of pop	GREAT BRITAIN Number	% of pop
2000	3,613,000	7.3	224,000	7.6	602,000	12.0	4,439,000	7.7
2005	3,166,000	6.3	200,000	6.7	511,000	10.0	3,877,000	6.6
2010	2,822,000	5.4	177,000	5.8	432,000	8.4	3,431,000	5.7
2015	2,474,000	4.6	150,000	4.8	382,000	7.5	3,006,000	4.9
2020	2,147,000	3.9	124,000	3.9	331,000	6.5	2,602,000	4.1
2025	1,824,000	3.3	100,000	3.1	260,000	5.1	2,184,000	3.4
2030	1,566,000	2.8	83,000	2.5	189,000	3.7	1,838,000	2.8

'Critical mass' is often taken as 5% – the smallest percentage of people who can significantly influence a nation. Church attendance falls below that by 2020, and is a long way below by 2030. We are indeed living in injury time.

Some would say the above figures are optimistic. Nick Page in his book *The Invisible Church* (see bibliography) considers that the church will be on the brink of disappearing by 2030 and will have disappeared altogether by 2040. Tom Horwood, who worked for the Catholic Bishops of England and Wales for 6 years, writes, 'If the trends of the last 40 years continue . . . the Catholic Church in Britain will barely exist in 2041.'[127]

Churches are getting smaller

The decline in the number of people is at a greater rate than the number of churches closing. Consequently the average size of congregations has dropped from 134 in 1980 to 80 in 2005, and adding this into Table 6.2, brings the number down to 47 by 2030.

Closure of churches

At some stage over the next 20 years this small average congregation size will mean that many churches will become financially unviable, and therefore will have to close. This is especially likely to be in rural areas, though small churches in inner city areas or on council estates may well face the same predicament. One researcher found closing churches 'to be in areas of higher population and greater population increase'.[128]

This raises the issue of mission to strategic areas, and how far key churches in such crucial areas should be supported either by central denominational funding, or perhaps by larger churches in the area acting as a kind of 'Minster' or mentor church and supporting their ministry.

Can Evangelical churches survive?

The results of the 1998 English Church Attendance Survey showed that Evangelicals in England at least had grown, even if those of other churchmanships or ethos had not.[129] However, the most recent research shows that while Evangelicals have declined less than others, this is solely because many black churches are growing, the large majority of which are Evangelical. (A 'black church' is the shortened form of 'Black Majority Church' – which means a majority of black people in the congregation.) If the Evangelical figures are broken down by ethnicity, as in Figure 6.3, it will be seen that white Evangelicals are declining at much the same rate as everyone else.

Figure 6.3: Change in English Church Attendance by Churchmanship, 1998–2005

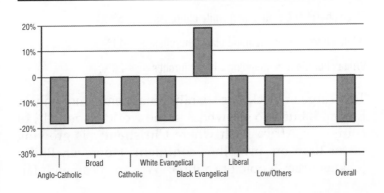

The importance of the black churches for the future of British Christianity is clear in a number of ways. We now turn to them.

2) Growth: the mustard seed grows into a great big tree

Jesus' parable of the mustard seed and the kingdom of heaven is a good analogy for the black churches (Matt. 13:31,32). They started out as tiny 50 years ago, and have grown much larger since, and seem likely to keep on growing.

Black church growth

The number of black churchgoers, of Caribbean and African descent, grew substantially in the 7 years 1998 to 2005. They were 10% of all churchgoers in 2005, up from 7% in 1998. While overall attendance was down –15%, this may be broken down as follows.

Black churchgoers attending black churches	+44%.
Black churchgoers attending white churches	+8%.
White churchgoers attending black churches	–11%.
White churchgoers attending white churches	–20%.

This surge in black Christianity is happening not only in England, but also elsewhere in the world, especially, of course, in Africa itself where Christianity is growing faster than on any other continent. However, Philip Jenkins urges a note of caution: 'We can speak with fair confidence about the ethnic composition of the world's Christians in 50 or 100 years, but we must be on shakier grounds when it comes to predicting attitudes to authority or orthodoxy.'[130]

The number of black churches is also growing, many started by individuals keen to reach their families and neighbours. Growth has occurred especially in London, where 25% of the capital's 4,100 churches are Pentecostal, the majority black.

Why are the black churches growing?

Jonathan Oloyede, a former Senior Pastor of Glory House, a multicultural church in East London, which regularly sees 3,000 or more on a Sunday, has outlined some reasons why black majority churches (BMC) grow.[131]

1 The church is the hub for community life.

2 Many black churches have a cosmopolitan outlook, not a parish mentality.

3 Black communities are very communal with a culture of visiting, socializing and regular personal interaction.

4 Black churches are very evangelistic and outreach driven.

5 The principle of tithe-giving helps financial buoyancy and independence.

6 Bible-based sermons are relevant to the congregation.

7 Services are vibrant, musical and worshipful.

8 Many black believers testify to experiencing healings and miracles.

9 Many BMCs have a home cell network, which facilitates strong pastoral care.

10 Sunday schools are usually a norm and part of weekly worship.

11 The dynamics of many BMCs facilitate lay leaders' training.

12 Various departments and programmes allow large volunteer participation.

13 Prayer is the key focus in many BMCs.

14 BMCs lay good emphasis on business and career prospects.

15 BMCs have a culture of great respect and reverence for the clergy.

16 Many BMCs have youth clubs/activities that retain young people within the church community.

How many of these factors could be incorporated in helping white churches grow?

Reverse mission

Two centuries ago Britain sent many missionaries to countries such as Ghana and Nigeria. They are now sending missionaries to the 'motherland' to enable Britain to return to the gospel and faith it used to have. (This is being mirrored currently in Brazilian Christians going to Portugal.) Black church denominations are being started here deliberately to win the British to

Christ. Some of these are remarkably successful, like the (Nigerian) Redeemed Christian Church of God, which numbered over 140 congregations in 2007 (many of which have white people among them).

The Ghanaian Deeper Life Church has also started several congregations. Their membership requirements are high. You have to be born again, showing over a six-month period a mature and lively Christian faith, the ability to speak in tongues and to answer positively (preferably in a short timeframe) the question, 'When did God last answer your prayer for a miracle?'

This reverse mission movement is likely to continue and expand in the years ahead.

Other non-white growth

The growth of the black churches has captured the attention of the media, but other non-white ethnic groups are also growing. Collectively they amounted to 7% of total churchgoers in England in 2005, up from 5% in 1998. That growth is shared as follows.

Chinese, Korean and Japanese	3% increase to 56,000
Indian, Pakistanis and Bangladeshis	9% increase to 59,000[132]
Singaporeans, Filipinos and other Asians	24% increase to 45,000
Latin Americans and other non-whites	27% increase to 33,000

There is also growth in the white non-British European churches from all parts of Europe (such as the French, Spanish, Croatian, Hungarian, Polish, Swiss, Portuguese, Danish, Icelandic, Russian, etc.). Part of this growth is a reflection of Britain's immigration policy of welcoming many people to these islands, but part also is the affinity such groups have for their compatriots. For example, if you are a Croatian who struggles with English from Monday to Friday, you will gladly go to one of the 7 new Croatian churches started between 2000 and 2005 where your language is spoken, probably irrespective of whether you previously went to church regularly (though many immigrants do come from churchgoing cultures).

Fresh Expressions

Ever since the publication of Bishop Graham Cray's excellent book *Mission-shaped Church*,[133] the concept of new types of meetings specifically for mission has been popular in the UK. The idea has been taken forward in depth through the initiative of the Archbishop of Canterbury. He set up the Fresh Expressions organization, initially led by Steven Croft, and now by Graham Cray. It is defined on their website as

> A form of church for changing culture, established primarily for the benefit of people who are not yet members of any church.

The 2005 English Church Census approached some 200 of these groups, and received 40 replies – not enough for a definitive sample, but, at the time of writing, the only specific research about their size and make-up. The Census showed that Fresh Expressions were smaller than the average Anglican congregation (about 61 people), and made up of younger people (average age 29 instead of 45). Since then, Fresh Expressions have greatly expanded – more than 5,000 are listed on their website, the idea has spread to other denominations, and at least a further 3,000 Anglican churches are reported to be considering the idea. All this activity is excellent news.

However, even if 2,000 new Fresh Expressions are started every year, and, say, 90% are new churches, if half of those coming are new people, then that means 30 new people at 1,800 new churches each year. Suppose 10 of these 30 people are aged 15 to 19, then that means 18,000 new teenagers each year. That compares with the average loss of 15,000 15 to 19 year olds to the church in Great Britain every year. The challenge to really grow is daunting when you look at the immensity of the task. Some would say that the threshold of new churches being started (with sufficient structure behind them to support them) is 2% of a denomination's size, so by that standard the Church of England is secure.[134] Secure, however, is not the same as flourishing.

Growing churches

In 2005, 34% of English churches had grown[135] over the previous 7 years (about 13,000 churches), compared with 21% in 1998 (or about 8,000 churches). An extra 5,000 growing churches is good news. It reflects, in part, the emphasis being made to help leadership in many denominations think ahead and make action plans for the future. Perhaps, though, it reflects even more the developing hunger among God's people in this country to see him work in an awesome and mighty way in this land. The sad news, however, is that most of this growth comes from people moving from their existing church to join a church which they feel suits them better. Less than 30% of new people joining the average church are people who are new to the faith.

Part of the growth in a church is 'biological', that is, it comes from churchgoing mothers having babies. From the Census giving the ages of women at church and the published government fertility rates it is possible to estimate the number of babies born to churchgoing mothers in a typical year, assuming that churchgoing women have children at the same rate as non-churchgoing women. Between 1998 and 2005 that averaged about 14,000 babies a year in England, or two babies for every five churches.

Youth activity midweek

Only a quarter, 27%, of churches have some kind of weekday youth activity. Most of these are among the growing churches. Many families move church in order to join one where their children can attend a midweek youth club of some kind, with the hope they will make Christian friends, and receive Christian teaching rarely available in our schools now, and so remain in a church context for longer.

So while some movements from one church to another reflect consumerism, choosing a church 'which suits me better', other such movements are deliberately strategic. Churches involved in other types of midweek activity, such as for the local community, are often growing too. Hope 2008 was one well-publicized popular activity that helped involve both younger and older people in community projects near their church, extending its caring image. This has sometimes led to new people coming.

One growing church, for example, at the beginning of a new pastor's ministry, sent a questionnaire around the local community asking what they would like from their church. The replies 'keep our children off the streets and provide for our old people' have been an integral part of that church's vision ever since – and the church is flourishing.

Conversions

People are being converted in Britain, many through teaching courses such as 'Alpha', 'Emmaus' or 'Christianity Explored'. From an analysis of Alpha surveys, it is possible to calculate the number of people joining the church after coming to faith.[136] Conversions through non-Alpha teaching courses are at about the same rate, but collectively only half as many since Alpha runs twice as many courses as all the others put together. Between 1998 and 2005 some 150,000 people started attending church as a consequence of attending teaching courses, and a further 100,000 for other reasons.[137]

Occasional Offices

One small but effectual means to growth in a few churches, especially where there are many Polish immigrants, is the opportunities provided by what the Anglicans call 'Occasional Offices' – baptisms, marriages and funerals.[138] Two-fifths (39%) of parents had their babies christened or baptized as infants in 2008.[139]

Three-fifths (60%) of the 245,000 marriages in England and Wales in 2005 were first marriages, and half (46%)

were celebrated in a place of worship.[140] There were
479,400 deaths in England in 2005, 43% having a Church
of England funeral, and another 30% a funeral by
another denomination.[141]

These are significant numbers and given that each such
event is attended by several, sometimes dozens, of
family members and friends, the overall numbers
contacted are considerable. Churches use these
opportunities in various ways. 'People may live more
secular lives, but they retain sacred hearts.'[142]

Christmas

Another area of growth is interesting: church attendance
at Church of England Christmas services has increased
15% between 2000 and 2006, with 3 million people going
in 2006.[143] Christmas churchgoers are 40% Anglican,
compared with 28% attending on an average Sunday,
giving the Church of England very special opportunities
to reach these annual churchgoers.

3) The age profile of current churchgoers is extremely serious

Just before he took the young people's slot in the
morning service at a suburban church on 4 February
2007 the speaker asked the congregation to continue
standing as they finished the preceding hymn. He then
asked all those alive on the occasion of England's last
World Cup soccer win in 1966 to sit down. At least 80%
of the congregation did so and there were gasps all
round the building. Such an age profile is typical of
thousands of churches.

Figure 6.4: Age of Churchgoers in Great Britain, 1980 to 2020

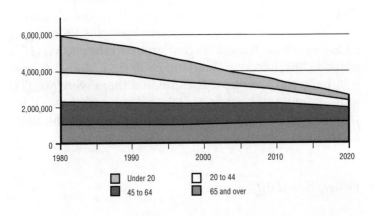

Figure 6.4 is based on the findings of the various Church Censuses and assumes present trends continue to 2020. In 1980 there were over 2 million people under the age of 20 in church across Great Britain; by 2020 that number will be under 240,000. Our young people have been decimated in 40 years.

More elderly people

One of the consequences of the numbers shown in Figure 6.4 is that the proportion of those 65 and over increases from 19% in 1980 to 46% by 2020. While any congregation may grow, research has shown that those with none or very few people under the age 40 have much greater difficulty.[144]

Many grandparents

One feature of the current age profile of the church is that Third Agers (the government term for those aged 65 to 74) are the largest 10-year group in the church (17% of total churchgoers in England in 2005[145]). Many of these will be grandparents: it is estimated there were 800,000 grandparents in church in 2005.[146] How can these older people best be used for the kingdom while we still have them?

Generational differences

Figure 6.4 highlights the make-up of the different generations in the church. These differences have been described in much detail elsewhere,[147] but are summarized below for convenience.[148]

Table 6.5a: Generations of British People, Years of Birth

GENERATION	OTHER NAMES	YEARS OF BIRTH	AGE RANGE IN 2010	POPULATION SIZE IN 2010, UK
Seniors		1926 and earlier	84 and over	1.7 million
Builders	Boosters, Maturity	1927–45	65 to 83	8.8 million
Boomers	Baby Boomers	1946–64	46 to 64	15.3 million
Busters	Generation X	1965–83	27 to 45	15.9 million
Mosaics	Generation Y	1984–02	8 to 26	14.6 million
Kaleidoscopes	Generation Z	2003–21	7 and under	5.6 million

Table 6.5b: Generations of British People, 1940–2030

Name	1940	1950	1960	1970	1980	1990	2000	2010	2020	2030
Builders	Age 5 or under	Age 5–23	Age 15–33	Age 25–43	Age 35–53	Age 45–63	Age 55–73	Age 65–83	Age 75–93	Age 85–103
Boomers		Age 4 or under	Age 14 or under	Age 6–24	Age 16–34	Age 26–44	Age 36–54	Age 46–64	Age 56–74	Age 66–84
Busters				Age 5 or under	Age 15 or under	Age 7–25	Age 17–35	Age 27–45	Age 37–55	Age 47–65
Mosaics						Age 6 or under	Age 16 or under	Age 8–26	Age 18–36	Age 28–46
Kaleido-scopes							Age 7	Age 17 or under	Age or under	Age 9–27

One key aspect of the generational differences was highlighted by Charles Price, a British minister from the Peoples Church, Toronto.[149] He felt that whereas church culture used to be defined denominationally (such as an Anglican or Methodist) or socially (such as professional or working class), today's culture is defined generationally, so that the Boomer culture is different from the Gen X culture which again is different from the Gen Y culture. He went on to say that each culture has to be reached appropriately and targeted suitably.

Gavin Peacock, football pundit and television presenter, believes this can come about through skilfully embracing new technology 'without discarding the important elements of tradition'.[150] Some, like Roger Standing, lecturer at Spurgeon's Baptist College, believe that the boomer generation will return to church when they retire.[151] Others, like John Drane, Professor of Practical Theology at Aberdeen University, believe that in the search for meaning after September 11th, a re-invigorated style of ministry is needed.[152]

It would seem that research thus needs to be framed for reasonably narrow age-brackets. This is what the book *Making Sense of Generation Y* did, and caused a stir when it was published as it suggested that those aged 16 to 25 are more likely to follow a 'happy midi-narrative' (i.e. between a meta-narrative and a mini-narrative) in which God and the spiritual played very little part (see bibliography). It was based on interviews with 41 young people in this age group, it reached conclusions which were controversial by comparison with other research findings, and needs to be replicated to prove or disprove whether this group was exceptional or normal for their age.

Young people leaving church

British research has shown that many young people leave church either around the age they go to secondary school or when they complete it.[153] The prime reason given is that church is 'boring' (87%), but the fact that it isn't cool (73%), they can't be bothered (67%), they don't believe in God (64%), they have other things to do (63%), their friends don't attend (61%) and they don't get up in time (48%) are also all relevant.

American research has found that 70% of young churchgoers leave between the ages of 18 and 22, the age when many are at university. The main reasons given were life changes, and a lack of friends in the church, but starting work and moving away from their home church were also key factors.[154] Do young people who leave ever come back? Research undertaken in the early 1990s, both in England and America, found that in both countries about 40% did (albeit after an absence of 8 to 10 years).[155] This research desperately needs updating; I personally doubt such a high percentage will do so in the days ahead.

It is interesting that over the past few decades pressures on young people have increased immensely, not least in the domains of taking drugs, smoking, drinking and sexuality. Teenage sexual behaviour has radically changed with perhaps 38% of young women and 18% of young men no longer virgins at 16.[156] 'The increased levels of alcohol consumption amongst young people comprise some of the most alarming trends in the UK,' reports the respected Joseph Rowntree Foundation.[157] Perhaps it is no mistake 55% of adults think children today are less happy than they were as children. It is worth noting that The Good Childhood Inquiry found a positive role for religion and spirituality in the psychological health of children.[158]

Teenagers wouldn't often describe themselves as being disillusioned with church. Disillusionment, however, is a crucial factor; and some particularly struggle with how science and the Bible can appear to conflict. There is an ongoing debate surrounding school funding by religious organizations such as David Vardy's Emmanuel Schools Foundation, and whether they should be allowed to teach 'creationism'. Nevertheless, some, like Peniel Academy in Brentwood, are able to do so.

At the same time, the numbers of young people taking Religious Studies for their GCSE exam has increased from 99,000 in the UK in 1993 to 180,000 in 2008 (a number almost three times the estimated total of 63,000 16-year olds attending church or other faith institutions).[159]

Older people leaving church

Francis and Richter have researched those who leave church over a long period. Their first book on the subject, *Gone But Not Forgotten* (published 1998), was updated by a further study 10 years later in *Gone for Good*. They found 15 'discrete themes' for leaving, of which the main ones were disillusionment and irrelevancy, followed by being excluded by cliques (about half). These are the other key reasons:

- Churchgoing was part of growing up (two-fifths).
- Inadequate return for time and money (two-fifths).
- Moving to a new area or family commitments (a third).
- Loss of faith (a third).
- Worship too formal or informal, or teaching too high or low (a third).
- Tensions with work (a quarter).
- Minister was too authoritarian (Roman Catholic) or too unclear (Anglican) (a quarter).
- Church was too conservative (a quarter).
- Lack of boundaries between the church and the world (a quarter).
- Disliked change (e.g. new hymns) (one-fifth).
- Hurt by pastoral failure (14%).
- Church too feminine or too difficult for those sexually active outside marriage (minority).

David Beer of Purpose Driven Europe has also found that irrelevance is one of the fundamental causes of

British church decline and the consequent lessened influence of churches in their locality.[160] 'Concerns for power and relevance are more obvious than concern for piety and faithfulness,' retorts Os Guinness (of the Trinity Forum, Washington DC).[161]

Age of leaders

It is often said that a church minister tends to attract people to the church within roughly plus or minus 10 years of his or her age, though there is no known British research to back this up. With the average age of a minister at 54 in 2005, that would suggest most folk joining the church would be between 44 and 64.[162] Unfortunately the age of those joining is also not known (though, according to some sources, the average age of conversion is 14).

The Church of England is the only denomination which regularly publishes the age of its clergy: the number over 50 is increasing. In 1994 the proportion of those recommended for ordination training who were 50 or over was 14% of the total; by 2005 this had increased to 34%.[163] If there are fewer younger people, then the natural ability to attract younger people into the church may be more limited. If there are fewer younger leaders, how can sufficient numbers get the necessary experience before they reach retirement in order to be promoted to archdeacons or bishops?

In addition the number of part-time ministers is increasing, not only in the larger, established denominations, but also in the burgeoning number of black churches.

The Church of England is also the only denomination which regularly publishes the gender of its ministers. The number and proportion of female ministers has been steadily increasing. In the year 2000 there were 1,140 female ministers, 12% of the total. By 2006, that had increased to over 1,500, 18% of the total, and an increase of 35% in 6 years against a male decline of –16% in the same period.[164] Female ministers are much more likely to be liberal than male clergy, 38% to 25% in 2005, and less likely to be Evangelical, 15% to 23%.[165]

The age of the leader is also important for growth. More leaders in their 40s see their church grow than leaders of other ages.[166] Length of stay matters as well. 'While five-year contracts are introduced for the clergy, nobody seems aware that churches grow only if their ministers stay for ten years.'[167]

4) Changing family life

'Married couples are no longer the social norm' ran the headlines when the latest results of the British Social Attitudes survey report was published in 2008.[168] This is probably the biggest change concerned with marriage in the last 20 years, even the last 20 centuries!

Cohabitation common, and increasing rapidly

In 1998 some 8% of those 16 and over in England and Wales were cohabiting, a percentage which had more than doubled to 19% just five years later. As Figure 6.6 indicates the greatest increase was among those aged 35 to 44, while the greatest number who cohabit, over a third, are those aged 25 to 34.

Figure 6.6: Proportions Cohabiting in England and Wales, 1998 and 2003, by Age

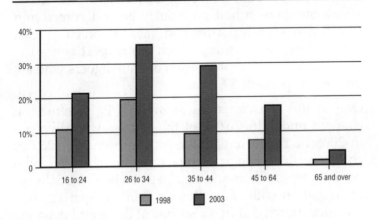

Several studies undertaken between 1999 and 2001 suggested that 2% of churchgoers were cohabiting.[169] A survey in one large church in 2008 gave the same percentage. With over two-thirds, 70%, of the population seeing nothing wrong with sex before marriage (48% in 1984),[170] the church has to find ways of accepting and welcoming people living in such relationships, while not abandoning the scriptural stance on marriage.

No longer marriage to one person for life

While the ideal has always been 'until death do us part' for marriage, the number of divorces peaked in the early 1990s but has declined only very slightly since then, numbering 133,000 in 2006, less than in 1991 (159,000) because there are fewer marriages. This is equivalent in 2006 to roughly one person in 40 in the population divorcing.

In 2006, there were 237,000 marriages. Of these, 144,000 were to people both marrying for the first time, 50,000 where one person had previously been divorced and 43,000 where both parties had been divorced at least once before, proportions which are respectively 61%, 21% and 18%.[171] The proportion of churchgoers who are divorced is perhaps 3%.

One of the consequences of divorce is its effect on children under 16. 70,000 of the couples who divorced in 2006 had children under 16, representing 125,000 children. Remarriage brings together children who become step-brothers and step-sisters who do not always easily get on with each other or their step-parent. This includes church children also; one of the useful debating subjects for the youth club might be 'coping with step-siblings'. Another is enabling those aged 10 to 14 especially to know how to cope when their parents divorce – the relationship with grandparents is often important in holding their world together. What model of marriage can children learn to emulate?

Divorce or cohabitation separation results in an increasing number of lone parents. In 2004 there were 13.1 million 'family' households; of these 73% were married couples, 15% cohabiting couples and 12% lone parents. By 2016, the government estimates these percentages will be, respectively, 66%, 21% and 13%.[172] The proportion of lone parents in society is far, far greater than the proportion of lone parents in most churches.

What does 'family' mean?

Two surveys asked children how they defined a family. The results were almost identical.

- Any group who care about you deeply: 56%.
- Where all the members are related to each other: 37%.

Children were also asked how they would define 'home'. They said home is a place where . . .

- I feel secure and loved: 59%.
- Sometimes I feel loved, other times I don't: 24%.

Church children affected

A 2005 survey of churchgoing children asked who they lived with.[173] The results are shown in Figure 6.7:

Figure 6.7: Marital Relationship of Parents of Churchgoing Children

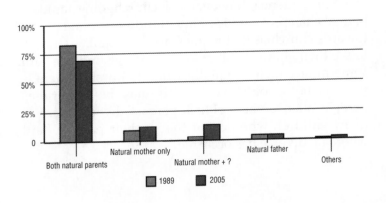

It may be seen that only two-thirds of churchgoing children were growing up with both natural parents, and that while there was a slight increase in lone mothers, the greater increase was when their natural mother had either remarried or was living with a new partner. When the minister asks children to bring 'their mum and dad' to the Christmas service, it must be remembered that for a third of church children their unspoken question is, 'Do you mean my real dad, my step-dad or the man currently in our house?'

A survey reported on CBBC (BBC's children's channel) found that quite young children, aged 6 to 12, cared more about doing well at school (32% described it as the most important thing in their life) than getting on with relatives (28%), having good friends (19%) or being good at sport (10%).[174] Perhaps school work seemed most important because 52% reported that school work dominated family conversations. The low priority of family must be, at least in part, due to the way family life is changing. It is interesting to note 25% of the children did not count their father as immediate family.

One consequence, however, for churchgoing families, both of changing families, and attitudes of young people towards church, is that many Christian families struggle to see their children following the parents in their faith, something which is equally true of church leaders as well as lay people. While this may be sometimes, perhaps often, because of their parents' divorce, there are many children who do not follow their parents' faith where no divorce has occurred.

Both parents working

The percentage of women in the employment market has increased over the last 4 decades, from 59% in 1971 to 73% in 2007, and, of the 27% not employed, only 5% were unemployed, meaning that 22% were choosing not to work, either because they were ill, or caring for others, or looking after children.[175] In another government publication, 57% of families with children had both parents working, and 27% one parent working.[176] Can churches help stretched families by running breakfast or after-school clubs?

Churches' volunteer work has traditionally been undertaken by women during the week. Much of this service is no longer available now so many are out at work, and churches have increasingly had to employ full-time people for their community activities to run smoothly.

Having children later

The average age of marriage has increased because so many initially cohabit – in 2006 it was 32 for men and 30 for women against 26 and 23 respectively in 1961.[177] Women are also choosing to have their first child later, and not necessarily when they are married. In 2006, the number of women who became pregnant when aged 40 or over was almost double the number in 1996, and 44% of births were outside marriage.[178] These trends appear to be less true of church marriages.

Greenshifting

One unexpected development in family life has been of great benefit to a few rural churches. In the first four years of the twenty-first century some 352,000 people 'greenshifted', that is, they moved from urban or suburban life.[179] Some of these ended up in very remote rural areas like Herefordshire, Ryedale in North Yorkshire or Boston in Lincolnshire, all officially designated 'Remote Rural', coming in sufficient numbers to cause church attendance to grow in these areas. The proportion of children under 11 in church was highest in the remote rural areas of England.[180] An influx of young families into a small village church drastically changes its life.

There is no doubt that some of these trends are important for church life, but, as someone has said, 'detecting what is weather and what is climate in the swirl of the socio-cultural day-to-day gets harder'.[181] Sifting them in a church's sphere of ministry, guided by the Spirit, becomes ever more crucial.

5) The size of a church is becoming a critical factor

One of the analyses that can be made from church censuses is counting how many churches there are of different size congregations. The shift in size over 16 years is shown in Figure 6.8, where the 5,700 Roman Catholic churches have been excluded, because so many of their churches are very large, and, if included, would give a misleading view of the more sizeable churches:

Figure 6.8: Size of English Protestant Church Congregations, 1989 and 2005

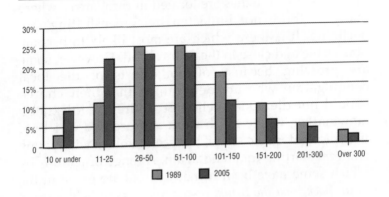

Figure 6.8 may be divided into four broad groups:

- The very small churches, 25 or under, whose numbers have risen dramatically, and are a third (31%) of all Protestant churches – almost 10,000 in total.

- The churches with between 26 and 100 people, many with just one ordained staff member, whose proportions have remained much the same over these 16 years, and who number almost half the churches (46%) – about 14,500 churches.

- The churches with between 100 and 200 people, also often with just one ordained staff member, whose number has shrunk to just 17% of all the churches, or 5,500 churches. They numbered 10,000 in 1989.

- The remaining large churches, some 6% of the total, or 2,000 churches with congregations in excess of 200.

The very small churches

Most of these churches are located in rural areas, where many of those not impacted by 'greenshifting' are declining. It is these which are most likely to become non-viable and close in the years ahead. However, some are growing because of the efforts of the local congregation who are determined that their church should not die. One such is St Andrew's, Mickfield, Stowmarket, where much work and use of a variety of worship and music styles, has seen families with young children starting to attend again. A range of reasons by which some have been turned around are given in the book *Back from the Brink*; resource books to help a small church also exist.[182] A good description of the problems of rural churchgoing is given in an article by Jill Bonser – such as driving down ice-prone roads with soft margins and deep drainage ditches for several miles![183]

The churches with between 100 and 200 people

Two-fifths, 38%, of these churches are in suburban or other built-up areas and a further fifth, 20%, in towns. A further one in seven, 14%, are in commuter rural areas. In 1974, David Wasdell showed that the average minister could remember 150 to 170 names of individual people, and that for a church to grow a second person was needed about the time that the congregation reached 150 to 200.[184] With that person appointed (whether a curate, an administrator or a youth director did not matter, simply someone to share the workload), many churches grew to up to 300 people.

However, such extra leadership is difficult to acquire as many churches in this size band lack the resources to appoint such a person. The number of volunteers dries up because so many are working. People leave to join more thriving (and invariably larger) churches: denominational or churchmanship loyalty is not strong, but the consumerist approach to church life is. Many people have cars and are happy to travel up to 5 miles to go to a church they like. Two-thirds, 70%, of suburban churches have ministers who are 50 or over.

Hence many ministers of these churches find it hard to meet the expectations of their congregation despite working many hours to do so. They are conscious of many opportunities, but do not always have the energy or resources to meet them, or the time to strategically plan which are the greatest priorities to focus on. As Figure 6.8 suggests, in many ways these are perhaps the most vulnerable churches after the very small ones.

Larger churches: types

The Americans make much of 'megachurches', defined as those with congregations in excess of 2,000 people. The English equivalent is probably churches with 400 or more. One book has divided the American megachurches into the following types.[185]

- The traditional church which has been around for many years but has grown substantially.

- The specialized 'seeker' churches (ones where services are entirely geared to outsiders – Willow Creek and Saddleback are probably the best known).

- The charismatic or Pentecostal type churches (which equate in part to some of the black churches in the UK).

- The innovative churches, some of which have been brilliantly successful in the States (and perhaps some of the UK's Fresh Expressions will equally grow very large over time).

The book suggests that these are in the proportions 30%, 30%, 25% and 15% in the States, but in the UK they would be radically different, perhaps 65%, 5%, 25% and 5% respectively. About five-sixths, 83%, of UK large churches and 95% of US ones are Evangelical.[186]

Larger US churches: myths

The same book lists various 'myths' about larger churches, which the authors debunk chapter by chapter. Many ministers of the larger churches in the UK would say they apply here also.

- 'All megachurches are alike.'

- 'That church is just too big!'

- 'Megachurches are cults of personality.'

- 'These churches are only concerned about themselves and the needs of their attendees.'

- 'Megachurches water down the faith.'

- 'These churches are bad for other churches.'

- 'These churches are full of people of the same race, class and political preferences.'

- 'Megachurches grow because of the show.'

- 'The megachurch movement is dying – young people hate these churches.'

These myths can all be debunked in the British scene as well. David Beer, minister of 800-strong Frinton Free Church for many years, writes, 'A large church can have a caring heart and a sense of belonging without everybody necessarily knowing each other.'[187]

Larger UK churches: their significance

There are perhaps 500 Protestant churches with average Sunday congregations of 350 or more in England: 170 Church of England, 60 Baptist, 20 Independent, 100 new churches and 150 Pentecostal (including the black churches). In addition there are some 1,300 Roman Catholic churches of this size. These larger Church of England churches, 1% of all their churches, were responsible for about 10% of the total Church of England congregations in 2005, up from 5% in 1989, and likely to be 15% by 2015. Likewise, the largest 2% of Baptist churches saw 10% of their collective congregations in 2005.

Collectively, the largest 5% of churches account for about a third, 30%, of all church attenders, the next quarter, 25%, of churches see almost half, 45%, of churchgoers and the large number of smaller churches have the remaining quarter of churchgoers. These proportions are illustrated in Figure 6.9:

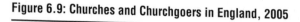

Figure 6.9: Churches and Churchgoers in England, 2005

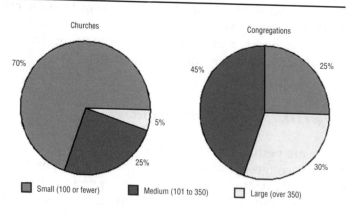

Churches

70%

5%

25%

Congregations

45%

25%

30%

☐ Small (100 or fewer)   ■ Medium (101 to 350)   ☐ Large (over 350)

These larger churches are clearly of strategic significance for the future of the church in the UK. In general society, the dominance of a small number of really big businesses is becoming quite common, and church life is following the same pattern. A leader at Highfields Free Church, Cardiff, says, 'We are very privileged. How do we best use what we have?' This stewardship is from God.

One example of their impact is the overseas mission support they can offer.

• A fifth, 20%, of small churches (25 or under) support a mission worker overseas.

• Two-fifths, 40%, of churches of 25 to 150 do so.

• Two-thirds, 65%, of churches of 151 to 250 do so.

• 100% of churches of over 250 support at least one.

Larger churches: why they grow

Why churches grow has been the subject of numerous books. Some of the key reasons are: strong leadership, clear vision,[188] relevant preaching, warm welcome, friendly congregation and a variety of worship/music styles. Some of these have been measured explicitly in a larger church context.

- The relevance of the teaching: 91%.

- Enthusiastic worship: 83%.

- The activities of the church: 82%.

- The warm welcome received: 80%.[189]

A factor common to many larger churches is they attract more of those who may find it difficult to attend smaller churches, such as single-parent families and divorced people. In a large church they are present in sufficient numbers to form their own group of friends in similar circumstances.

Larger churches often have a well-trained welcome team. I was asked to evaluate the welcome given to strangers in one large church some distance from London. When I attended, the lady in charge that day looked me straight in the eye, said, 'Good morning, welcome to St Michael's. Have you been here before?' When I said I hadn't she replied, 'We're so glad you're able to join us today and trust you'll enjoy your time with us. These are the books you will need. Feel free to sit wherever you like. That gentleman over there will show you to a seat if you wish.' I gave them 10 out of 10. I had been made to feel at home.

In a large Baptist church in Kent, a couple attending for the first time went through the entrance and were immediately asked if they'd like a cup of coffee. The wife in the family in front turned to the couple, asked if they'd been before, and, discovering it was their first visit, immediately invited them to lunch.

An Anglican minister, knowing a Christian family was moving into his parish, called in on moving day, saying, 'I know you're very busy just now. Just wanted to welcome you in the Lord's name to this town. Here's my card: contact me if you need me,' and was gone within two minutes. That family joined his church for 36 years, until they moved home.

Larger Churches: *why they keep people*

One survey asked those who had started attending a large church within the last year, why they continued to come.[190] Their replies, in descending order of importance, were:

- Opportunity to grow spiritually (more women than men).

- Convenience – near to where I live.

- Regularly sense God's presence in worship (more younger people than older).

- Helpful teaching (more men than women).

- Inspiring worship (more men than women).

- Friendly people (more women than men; more younger people than older).

- Appropriate activities for my family (more younger people than older).

- Caring congregation (more women than men).

Some large churches have undertaken surveys of their congregation in order to understand better the dynamics of church life and so that the leaders can plan the most strategic way ahead. Anglican churches like Christ Church, Clifton, Baptist churches like Tonbridge Baptist, and Independent churches like Above Bar, Southampton, are all known to have done this in the last 3 years, for example.

6) The frequency of churchgoing is decreasing

One problem affecting churches of all sizes is that even regular attenders are coming less often. Some of the reasons have already been mentioned – more women are working; families are more dysfunctional; people find church less relevant, etc. These are valid reasons – if more families have both parents working, Saturday becomes a hectic household day with shopping, cleaning, washing and so on, to be fitted in, and Sunday becomes the only 'family' day for visiting, playing sport, or just chilling out. That is if the mother is working during the week – she may be at work on Sunday when father can provide childcare, and jobs are available in care or retail.

One leader in a youth organization wrote how he and his family faced up to this challenge before the Lord, and decided that keeping the family together was more important than attending church under compulsion. As a consequence they started attending once a month instead of every week, supporting their teenage son in his football on a Sunday morning, and have found that not only have the church leaders understood and accepted their decision, but his children now enjoy going to church because they know their parents accept and understand their position also.[191] Reacting to changing family circumstances in other ways can equally be a common reason for going to church less frequently.

Less frequent by age

The 2005 English Church Census found that frequency of attendance varied by age as Figure 6.10 shows:

Figure 6.10: Frequency of church attendance by age

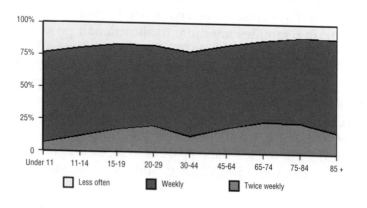

It is obvious that those aged 30 to 44 find it especially difficult. When a similar result was found in the 2002 Scottish Church Census, focus groups showed that the combination of having a home, a family to look after, work and church was frequently too great, and church was the only optional feature. While women are in the majority of those who left the church at every age, the proportion of women aged 30 to 44 who left between 1998 and 2005 was almost three-quarters, 72%, of women that age. 'Left' in this context does not usually mean quitting for good, but rather turning regular, say, weekly, attendance into less frequent attendance, say, monthly.

'The Sandwich Trap'

One of the pressures, especially upon women in their 40s or early 50s, is that while they still have teenage children at home, their own parents are getting increasingly frail, needing their care and help. A letter from a mother in this situation published in a national paper drew a huge response from readers, who called it 'the Sandwich Trap'.[192] One URC church in Kent recognized this as an issue and put on a morning conference entitled 'The Time of Your Life: Are you a woman who is trying to get the balance right in meeting the needs of your grown up children, elderly relatives and other significant relationships, as well as trying to find time for you?' Pressure to go to church will be part of that overall equation as well.

Those who drop out

Some, of course, do stop attending church altogether. Sometimes this is when people move and are unable or do not try to find another church they like. Some people leave because they lose their faith. The work of Francis and Richter in this context has already been quoted above. The consequence, however, is that the make-up of the population is rather curious.

7% go to church at least once a month.

8% go to church just once a year.

25% used to go, but now have stopped going.

32% call themselves Christian, but have never gone.

28% belong to another faith, are non-Christian or didn't answer the census question.

The numbers of ex-church (or de-churched) people in the country, some 15 million people, thus considerably exceeds the numbers who attend, if only once a year, at 9 million. *It is therefore as important to stop people leaving as to get them converted and attending church.* If some of those who had left came back to church some of our decline would be halted.

Back to Church Sunday

This was the idea of the Bishop of Manchester, the Rt Revd Nigel McCulloch, in 2004. He asked that all the churches in his diocese had an 'Open Sunday' instead of normal services on the last Sunday in September. Most complied and, as consequence, helped by a 'goodie bag' supplied with Co-op fair trade chocolates, some 6,000 extra people turned up.[193] The idea has since spread to other dioceses in the Church of England and to other denominations. *The Baptist Times* gave it front page attention in 2008. In 2006 some 20,000 extra people across the various Church of England dioceses came to church on Back to Church Sunday, and, six months later, some 8,000 of these were still coming to church, rather less than the 50% response in the original Manchester experiment, but very welcome nonetheless. The

Tearfund Awareness Monitoring Survey (done in 2008) found 25% of respondents willing to come back to church if invited.

Weekday activities

Two-fifths, 42%, of churches have some kind of mid-week devotional activity. For some this is a service, for many others a home group. These are an important way of deepening fellowship, extending pastoral care, and enabling better discipleship. In general they are popular as the number attending them is increasing at about 10,000 a year.[194] These are an important way of helping the church to grow on Sundays as well.

Some of the weekday events are youth activities of various kinds, demanding more helpers now since the implementation of Child Protection. About one church in five, 20%, now employs either a youth worker or a children's worker (sometimes called a families' worker) or both. There is an increasing phenomenon of volunteer helpers opting out as new 'professional' staff are appointed. Jason Gardner, LICC's Youth Project Researcher, says, 'I heard from a couple of newly appointed youth workers, both of whom had found that their arrival . . . served as catalyst for those who had previously been involved in the young people's work to relinquish their responsibilities in that area.'[195] Other churches have found exactly the same thing. This partly happens because people undervalue their own contribution as 'amateur' and are not aware of the value of their experience. Churches appointing new staff need to be aware of this danger and look for ways to minimize it.

Loss of spirituality

Eddie Gibbs's research in the early 1990s found that those who left the church and subsequently returned 'had lost out in key areas of discipleship'.[196] The late Henri Nouwen said, 'I've yet to meet anyone who has come closer to Jesus by forsaking the Church. To listen to the Church is to listen to the Lord of the Church'.[197]

7) The need to view the wider picture

The Langham Partnership is an international organization with headquarters in London. It seeks to provide selected men and women from the Majority World with quality theological education. In the autumn of 2007 it ran an advertisement in the Christian press, 'The church is growing fast', which, in the context of declining church attendance in Britain, read oddly. They meant the church outside 'the West', which is indeed growing noticeably quickly.

The rise of Majority World Christianity

During the last quarter of the twentieth century the number of Christians in 'the West' (the continents of Europe, North America and Australasia) became less than the number in the Majority World (the continents of Africa, Latin America and Asia). Figure 6.11 indicates this and projects to 2030, assuming present trends continue.[198]

Figure 6.11: Number of Christians in First and Third Worlds, 1970 to 2030

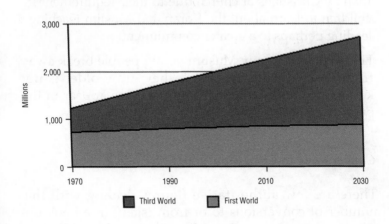

Why is there such growth? Philip Jenkins draws attention to two important phenomena which are seen more in the Third World than the First World: a huge number of people converting to Christianity through physical healing after prayer, and a deep belief in the Bible, the absolute Word of God.[199]

The growth of Islam

The number of Muslims is increasing in both the UK and worldwide. In the UK this is partly because of continuing numbers of immigrants, although exactly how many are Muslims is not known. It is also partly because of the 'biological' factor – Muslims have more children per family than families from any other religion. The average size of a Christian household is 2.3 people, whereas the average

Muslim one has 3.8 people.[200] There is probably a greater attendance at mosque by young people in Muslim areas than by Christians at church due to their requirement for children to learn about the Koran and Muslim teachings, leading perhaps to a greater commitment.

However, how many Muslim young people break away from their Muslim origins as they grow older is not known, although some high profile cases appear in the press from time to time.

Conversions to Christianity and vice versa

There are few authoritative figures dealing with the number of conversions to or from Islam. In a book on why women converted to Islam, the number of British converts to Islam is suggested at 3,000 per year in the 1990s.[201] This is lower than the number obtained from an analysis of the results of the Scottish population census of 2001, which puts it at about 5,000 a year.[202] Some would put the number even higher.

The number converting to Islam worldwide is not known with certainty either, nor are numbers converting the other way, that is, from Islam to Christianity. Numbers within Britain are thought to be fairly small, and certainly less than the number going the other way, but numbers converting from Islam to Christianity worldwide are thought to be in their thousands. One blog at least claims the numbers are in 6 figures.[203] A number describe many of the Muslim conversions as being due to personal dreams of Christ.

Others are describing the fact that many Muslims are converting to Jesus but staying within their Islamic culture. 'Someone from a Muslim background may follow Christ without having to leave his Arab and Islamic culture and community.'[204] (A whole series of articles devoted to this subject appeared in the *International Journal of Frontier Missions.*[205])

Growth and tension

While it is true that Christianity as a whole is growing across the world, it is only the Evangelical wing which is actually growing, and that only very slowly; liberals are static or declining. The only two religious groups in the world today showing increases are Islam and Evangelical Christianity. Muslims currently outnumber Evangelicals and are growing more strongly.[206] This is shown in the following diagram:

Figure 6.12: Comparison of Evangelical and Muslim growth as a percentage of world population, 1970–2030

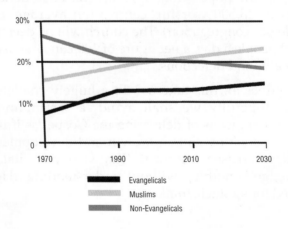

The fact it is the Evangelical and Muslim groups which are growing is likely to lead to clashes in the years ahead, and consequent suffering. It is already happening in African countries like Nigeria. One commentary on how to handle such trauma is given in a Crowther Monograph[207] and one of the issues of *Connections*.[208]

The wider Christian picture

In 2010 there are likely to be 2.3 billion Christians in a world of 6.9 billion people, 33%. Those Christians will be spread across 40,000 denominations in 3.8 million worship centres (so with an average of 600 people per congregation). The church will be increasing by 79,000 people per day, a net figure of 170,000 conversions less 91,000 deaths or defections. A quarter, 26%, of those Christians will be in Europe, where 'Christian' is defined as attending church at least once a year.[209]

In the UK, the equivalent figures are likely to be 7.7 million people attending church once a year in 2010, 12.5% of the population, spread across 310 denominations in 48,500 worship centres (an average of 160 people per congregation). The church will be decreasing by 240 people a day, a net figure of 100 conversions, less 340 deaths and defections.[210]

Where does all this take us? To a hugely challenging place! Hopefully we shall avoid 'a scrambling for prescriptive means of delivering the Gospel as if it's in the latest book on church growth and development'.[211] As one advertisement put it, 'Knowledge is vital, but knowledge is nothing without understanding'. Hence the need for strategic thinking.

Leadership is a fine balance between not taking action and taking action. Saul got it wrong in 1 Samuel 13 – told to wait for Samuel to come, he lost patience as his army began to slip away and took action when he should have had the faith to wait a while longer. Part of leadership is not just knowing what to do, but also knowing when to do it – the so-called *chairos* moment. Saul needed to know what and in whom his resources were, as shown in chapter 2. The present time is just as crucial. There is likely to be a net loss of 8,000 British churches in the next 20 years. The more we tarry, the larger the slippage. The scripture is unequivocal – *now* is the time . . .

7

WHO WE ARE

The following notes give a more detailed description of the various Belbin categories which were described in chapter 2. However, for a much more thorough evaluation of the meanings of each category, readers are recommended to read the basic book by Meredith Belbin, *Management Teams*.

A) Creatives

The major role of the Creative person in a team is to come up with new ideas and strategies. Creatives are the ideas people of the team, and their ideas may often be radical. They have masses of creative energy – and use it. The Creative is likely to come up with both original suggestions to problems and possible new solutions to long-standing issues.

Creatives take an independent and innovative look at most situations and will see patterns where most people will only see unconnected ideas. This gives the Creative the ability to rearrange ideas and ways of doing things, which often results in success. Creatives have lots and lots of ideas, more ideas before breakfast than many of us have in a week or a month. Without a Creative your team is going to be seriously lacking in imaginative ideas.

However, Creatives have weaknesses. Some of the suggestions will be totally impractical. Creatives tend to have their head in the clouds, no idea what day of the week it is, nor what time it is, so can easily forget appointments. Creatives have a tendency to disregard practical details, can be very critical of others, and can easily be trodden on. They can be extremely sensitive, so need protecting.

If there is more than one Creative in the team, then conflict can arise, because there will be too many ideas, and each will be giving very convincing reasons why their ideas should be followed.

B) Critics

Critics tend to be serious, sober-minded people: people who think things through carefully and are slow in making up their mind. They are quite likely to throw cold water on the Creative's ideas. Without a Critic, every idea might seem to be a good one, because the Creative will have good convincing reasons.

Critics see the implications of a course of action. They are unlikely to be imaginative or have much originality or inspiration: their real asset is in making shrewd judgements that will take all the factors into account and which will stop the team from going up the wrong path. And they are rarely wrong.

Usually Critics are the only team members able to hold their own in a debate with a Creative – and can be capable of getting a Creative to change his or her mind. The Creative and the Critic are both people who are concerned with ideas, and sometimes the two roles can be equally combined in one person.

C) Detail Person

This is the person who will ensure that the team finishes the tasks it starts – Belbin's name for him/her is Completer-Finisher. They are conscientious and hard-working, but are likely to be more of an introvert. They are very good at planning ahead, and make sure that nothing is overlooked.

This is a perfectionist with an eye for detail, who makes sure that plans are completed to their level of satisfaction, with every detail absolutely correct. They have lots of self-control and self-discipline, and worry about the time and the money which is being spent while making sure the job is done properly.

They are reluctant to let a matter go unfinished – there are occasions when a Detail Person will hold on too long, refusing to accept defeat even when a project is not worth pursuing any further.

D) Resourcers

Unlikely to be a great source of original ideas themselves, these are people who pick up fragments of ideas from all sorts of sources and make them work. In circumstances of imminent failure Resourcers will look for the valuable piece of information which will 'save the day'.

Resourcers are enthusiastic, probably extrovert, and have a natural curiosity. They are particularly adept at exploring resources outside the group and are uninhibited about finding out what they want to know by making good use of other people. They're opportunistic, tend to 'think on their feet', know everyone, have excellent interpersonal skills and are sociable and friendly. If you want something, they know where to get it. If you want something done, they know whom to contact. They've got books full of addresses and telephone numbers.

Someone described a Resourcer as 'the executive who is never in her room, and if she is, she's on the phone'. They're often late for meetings. However, their follow-through/delivery isn't always as good as it could be, and they're not that competent at getting new things started.

Detailed People and Resourcers tend to make good journalists.

E) Task Workers

Task Workers are disciplined, conscientious, dependent and stable, even when under pressure. They are people who have an orderly approach to work, like routine, and are excellent at implementing schemes others have devised. They are aware of their obligations, tough-minded, practical, tolerant of others (though not necessarily supportive of them), conservative and ace organizers, with plenty of common sense. They are hard-working with a lot of self-discipline.

They often tend to see the big picture, rather than just the detail, and will always keep the vision in mind. They will put the good of the organization before their personal desires. However, they don't respond easily to change and have a lack of flexibility.

F) Team Workers

The primary motivation of the Team Worker is the good of the team. They're the people who hold everyone together, who are often able to defuse conflict between other members. Team Workers get on well with most people, and they are interested in how people relate and communicate. They are encouragers of others, they tend to help people see their strengths and handle their problems. They are always ready to support decent suggestions and projects. They also know how to help people pull together.

Team Workers are good communicators: they are the ones who will listen to others, and yet not be critical of other team members. They tend to be perceptive and diplomatic. They put the group's needs above self-interest because they focus on team spirit. Team Workers will be good in a crisis – the sort of people who say 'Let's have a cup of tea'. They will try to insist on having social times together.

They are the ones most likely to reduce any tension that occurs, through a good-humoured remark or a word of encouragement. Their weakness is that they will avoid pressurized situations, will have a tendency to be indecisive in times of crisis, and may focus so much on people that they don't give sufficient attention to the task they are employed to do.

G) Directors

Directors are leaders who have strong interpersonal skills, which they use to achieve agreement in the team.

They tend to be trusting by nature, accepting people as they are, and are tolerant of others and of their ideas, without ever losing sight of the task or the time. They always know the skills and abilities of their people and are calm and unflappable, especially in the face of controversy. They are self-confident, self-controlled and dominant (without being overly aggressive).

Directors are able to accept all potential contributions to a discussion without prejudice, and can shut up the Resourcer or the Critic and protect the Creative at the right time. They will stop the discussion from being uncontrolled, and have an almost innate sense of bringing the right person into the discussion at the right time. They are the 'conductor of the orchestra', the one who knows how to make the best use of the resources which each team member can offer.

They make the ideal chairperson for meetings, but they are not particularly brilliant and are unlikely to be particularly creative. Their weaknesses are that they tend to be lazy if they can find someone else to do the work and may take the praise for a team effort.

H) Shapers

Shapers are outgoing, dynamic leaders, with a high need for achievement. They have tremendous drive and their motivation is to win at any cost. They tend to be practical people, who will galvanize others into action, chal-lenging inertia, ineffectiveness or complacency. They tend to be impatient, and want results. They have a strong influence on group decisions, and are willing to be unpopular to get their view across.

They're the ones who 'won't suffer fools gladly'. They tend to be pushy, perhaps aggressive, because only results satisfy them – they dislike too much talk. They need to get on with the job and have a strong need for control with the result that they are sometimes called 'slave-drivers'.

Their weaknesses are that they may over-react to disappointment, ignore personal relationships, be inclined to irritability and easily frustrated. A Shaper can disrupt a well-balanced team. Several Shapers in a team may be unproductive because interpersonal problems are likely to arise as a result of conspicuous frustration and open criticism of others.

POSTSCRIPT: HOW WE GOT HERE

Risk taking is part of successful leadership. James Tysoe, initially a Hoover salesman who became head of the new World Vision of Europe (WVE) in the seventies, was a risk taker. He had to be. WVE became a successful fund-raising charity, sponsoring many children in just a few years, and in 1983 Tysoe launched MARC Europe – and asked me to head it up. Neither of us really knew what it was about. I asked for a job description and was told it was 'to strengthen Christian leadership in Europe'. When I asked how that was to be accomplished I was told to get on with it, as I was the boss!

The work developed into three strands: undertaking 'big picture' research showing how the church was moving in a whole nation (using church censuses) to enable better strategic planning by Christian leaders; publishing books on Christian leadership and management (very common now, but not at all common in the mid-eighties) and also resource books like the *UK Christian Handbook*; and undertaking training events, such as seminars and conferences on management, leadership and research topics. The latter area proved extremely popular and in its heyday in 1990 MARC Europe was running a hundred training courses a year.

The main energy behind the training work was Dr David Cormack, who had felt the Lord calling him to use his experience as Head of Training at Shell International for the good of the church. He became the Director of Management Training at MARC Europe and over the next five years proceeded to develop a wide range of leadership seminars on topics like time management, vision building, team management, team building, conflict resolution, marketing your church and the pursuit of excellence. David was succeeded by Dr Bryn Hughes (who is still much in demand as a church management consultant).

David lectured at most of the courses he produced, and one day he listed 'The Five Questions of God'. It was simply an introduction to his vision building course and, to the best of my knowledge, he never elaborated on them in the way that I have in this book. They were given as an interesting starter in the first session.

MARC Europe closed in 1993 and was succeeded by Christian Research which had identical foundations. The intention of the new organization was to concentrate more on research, although we continued to produce the *UK Christian Handbook*. However, church leaders continued to ask us for training courses, and we felt we should meet that need, but using the existing staff of Christian Research rather than employing specialist trainers, which we couldn't afford. Thus it was that the then Assistant Director, Heather Wraight, and I facilitated many more such training events. One of these was a course on vision building.

We occasionally found that our various research clients wanted more than just the results and were asking for insights into how the answers could be applied within their church or organization. In time, this led to a new seminar on the interpretation of research and to another on what we then called 'Thinking Future', effectively a seminar on strategic thinking. This was further developed after hearing a lecture in 2002 by the Chief of the Armed Forces (as he became), Richard Dannatt, on strategy. At the same time, I was beginning to see the strategic importance of the larger British churches who, collectively, wielded a huge influence on churchgoing numbers. A long and extremely helpful chat with Rt Revd Mike Hill (now Bishop of Bristol) one Friday afternoon caused Christian Research to hold its first Staff College for leaders of larger Anglican churches.

All this developed our understanding of strategic thinking, which was encapsulated into a book called *Coming Up Trumps!* This was used as the textbook for a new seminar on the same subject. These seminars were held all over the country for three years. At some stage in these seminars I introduced the five 'God's Questions' that I had initially heard from David Cormack. David sadly died an untimely death from cancer in 2007.

During this time Christian Research was constantly being asked to help with church 'vision building' days, which we were always very glad to do. The five Questions formed a helpful framework for thinking through the issues with churches, partly aided by the Questions having a biblical starting point. This coincided with the realization that some of *Coming Up Trumps!* was too theoretical for some readers, and so, when I approached Mark Finnie, Publishing Director of Authentic (which had published it), he kindly encouraged me to write this further book. This book in its present form owes a great deal to Heather Wraight and my minister, Derek Hills, who both read the book in draft form and made many helpful suggestions and to Rose Dowsett who read it at proof stage. I am also deeply grateful to Alec Hitchins, Noel Ford and Chris Radley for permission to use their illustrations and cartoons.

So that's how we have come to be where we are. It is not quite the end of the story, however. Christian Research has now merged with the Bible Society, and no longer undertakes leadership seminars as hitherto. I have retired from Christian Research, set up Brierley Consultancy, and continue to do vision building seminars for churches, undertake relevant research, help facilitate larger church events with CPAS and to work with other organizations for seminars or conferences on strategy, as well as publishing material whenever appropriate.

I remain challenged by Mahatma Gandhi's words

> You Christians look after a document containing enough dynamite to blow all civilization to pieces, turn the world upside down, and bring peace to a battle-torn planet. But you treat it as though it is nothing more than a piece of literature.

Alison Morgan, who gives the above quotation in her book *The Wild Gospel*, says a couple of pages later, 'The word of God is not a product but an encounter, not a mail-shot but a seed, not information but the nucleus of life itself. And as it grows inside us, it changes us by the generative power of the Holy Spirit.'[212]

'God's Questions' is the name of the book because his Word gives us exactly that – by daring to use five such as chapter headings, without, I trust, being presumptive, my prayer is that they will be seen, not as just printed 'literature', but the very source of life-giving strategic change that the western church so desperately needs. The challenge is not just to strengthen leadership but to enable that leadership to take imaginative risks for our precious and infinitely worthwhile goal – the spread of the Lord's kingdom.

BIBLIOGRAPHY

Beer, D., *Building a Strategic Church* (Eastbourne: Kingsway, 2007)

Belbin, R.M., *Management Teams: Why They Succeed or Fail* (Oxford: Butterworth Heinemann, 1981)

Billings, A., *Secular Lives, Sacred Hearts: The role of the Church in a time of no religion* (London: SPCK, 2004)

Brierley, P., *Archdeacons in the early 21st century: research report* (London: Christian Research, 2004)

Brierley, P., *Church Growth in the 1990s: A Statistical Report* (London: Christian Research, 2000)

Brierley, P., *Coming Up Trumps!: Four Ways into the Future* (Milton Keynes: Authentic Media, 2004)

Brierley, P., *Grandparents are increasingly important in the survival of the church!* (London: Christian Research, 2007)

Brierley, P. (ed.), *Religious Trends* No 4, 2003/2004 with Census results for Scotland (London: Christian Research, 2003)

Brierley, P. (ed.), *Religious Trends* No 6, 2006/2007 with Census results for England (London: Christian Research, London, 2006)

Brierley, P. (ed.), *Religious Trends* No 7, 2007/2008 (Swindon: Christian Research, 2008)

Brierley, P., *Leadership, Vision and Growing Churches* (London: Christian Research, 2003)

Brierley, P., *Priorities, Planning and Paperwork* (London: MARC Europe, 1992)

Brierley, P., *Pulling out of the Nosedive* (London: Christian Research, 2006)

Brierley, P., *The Tide is Running Out* (London: Christian Research, 2006)

Brierley, P., *Vision Building* (London: Hodder and Stoughton, 1989)

Cray, G., *Mission-shaped Church* (London: Church House Publications, 2004)

Dayton, E.R., *Tools for Time Management* (Grand Rapids, MI: Zondervan, 1974)

Fleming Drane, O., *Spirituality to Go: Rituals and Reflections for Everyday Living* (London: Darton, Longman and Todd, 2005)

Francis & Richter, *Gone for Good* (Peterborough: Epworth Press, 2008)

Frost, R., Wilkinson, D. & Cox, J. (eds), *The Call and the Commission* (Milton Keynes: Paternoster, 2009)

Giaquinto, M., *Visual Thinking in Mathematics* (Oxford: Oxford University Press, 2007)

Guinness, O., *Prophetic Untimeliness: A Challenge to the Idol of Relevance* (Grand Rapids, MI: Baker Books, 2004)

Handy, C., *The Hungry Spirit* (London: Hutchinson, 1997)

Hill, C., *Flowers in the Cities: The extraordinary 'Diana Prophecy'* (London: Marshall Pickering, 1998)

Hollingshead, M. & Nguya, E., *Adventures in Tornado Valley* (London: Thames and Hudson, 2008)

Hybels, B., *Holy Discontent: Fueling the Fire that Ignites Personal Vision* (Grand Rapids, MI: Zondervan, 2008)

Jenkins, P. *The New Faces of Christianity: Believing the Bible in the Global South* (Oxford: Oxford University Press, 2006)

Johnstone, P. & and Mandryk, J., *Operation World* (Milton Keynes: Authentic Media, 2001)

Kendall, R.T., *Total Forgiveness* (London: Hodder and Stoughton, 2001)

Laird, D.A. & E.C., *The Techniques of Delegating* (London: McGraw-Hill, 1957)

Lawrence, J., *Growing Leaders: Reflections on leadership, life and Jesus* (Oxford: CPAS & Bible Reading Fellowship, 2004)

Longley, D. & Spearing, M. (eds.), *Tyne and Wear Christian Directory* (London: MARC Europe, 1986)

MacDonald, G., *Restoring Your Spiritual Passion* (Crowborough, East Sussex: Highland Books, 1987)

Martin, P., *The Christian Charities Handbook* (Nottingham: IVP, 2008)

Morgan, A., *The Wild Gospel* (Oxford: Monarch Books, 2004)

Moynagh, M. & Worsley, R., *Tomorrow* (London: LexiCon Editorial Services, 2000)

Myra, H. & Shelley, M., *The Leadership Secrets of Billy Graham* (Grand Rapids, MI: Zondervan, 2005)

Naisbitt, J. & Aburdene, A., *Re-inventing the Corporation* (London: Guild Publishing, 1985)

New, G. & Cormack, D., *Why did I do that?: Understanding and Mastering your Motives* (London: Hodder and Stoughton, 1997)

Olson, D., *The American Church in Crisis* (Grand Rapids, MI: Zondervan, 2008)

Overman, C., *Assumptions that Affect Our Lives: How World Views Determine Values that Influence Behaviour and Shape Culture* (Washington: Ablaze Publishing, 2006)

Page, N., *The Invisible Church* (Grand Rapids: Zondervan, 2004)

Ross, S. & Carlson, C., *Say Yes to Your Potential* (Waco, TX: Word Books, 1983)

Rush, M. *Burnout* (Aylesbury: Scripture Press, 1989)

Savage, S. et al, *Making Sense of Generation Y* (London: Church House Publishing, 2006)

Sookhdeo, R., *Stepping into the Shadows: Why women convert to Islam* (Pewsey: Isaac Publishing, 2007)

Standing, R., *Re-Emerging Church: Strategies for reaching a returning generation* (Abingdon: BRF, 2008)

Thieve, E. R., *The Mysterious Numbers of the Hebrew Kings* (Grand Rapids: Zondervan, 1983)

Thumma, S. & Travis, D., *Beyond Megachurch Myths* (San Francisco: John Wiley and Sons, 2007)

Townsend, A. *Mid-Life Crisis* (Christchurch, New Zealand: Christian Value Books, 2008)

Verwer, G., *Out of the Comfort Zone* (Carlisle: OM Publishing, 2000)

Williams, R., *Marxism and Literature* (Oxford: Oxford University Press, 1977)

Wraight, H. & P., *Back from the Brink* (Worthing: Verité & London: Christian Research, 2006)

NOTES

GOD'S QUESTIONS

Chapter 1: Where Are You?

[1] Brierley, *Vision Building*.

[2] A seminar held in Kisumu at the request of the Diocese of South Maseno in 2005.

[3] Basic information allowing such comparisons may be found in the *Religious Trends* No 6, 2006/2007 for England and *Religious Trends* No 4, 2003/2004 for Scotland.

[4] Based on figures in Table 9.2 of *Pulling out of the Nosedive*, p. 190. The 'past position' describes church attendance change between 1989 and 1998 and 'current position' change between 1998 and 2005.

[5] The number added to the church from conversions and births between 1998 and 2005 was 350,000, averaging 50,000 a year or 500,000 across 10 years (figures from Brierley, *Pulling out...*, p. 203).

[6] Such as *The Success Principles: How to get from where you are to where you want to be,* Jack Canfield; *What should I do with my life?*, P. O. Branson; *Now, discover your strengths*, Marcus Buckingham and Donald Clifton; *Success built to*

last: Creating life that matters, Jerry Porras et al; *What Color Is Your Parachute?*, Richard Nelson Borres; *Winning: The Answers*, Jack and Suzy Welch; *The 8th Habit: From effectiveness to greatness*, Stephen R. Covey, etc. All these were described in an article 'Book in for success' by Steve Hart, *Weekend Herald*, New Zealand (19 April 2008).

[7] Quoted in the *Church of England Newspaper* (30 May 2008) speaking at the 2008 UK Christian Book Awards event, May 2008.

[8] Williams, *Marxism and Literature*.

[9] Wraight & Wraight, *Back from the Brink*.

[10] From Revd Tom Houston, one-time International Director of World Vision.

[11] Email (11 February 2008), quoted with permission.

[12] Such as the small pocket-sized booklet produced under the auspices of the National Council for Voluntary Organizations called *Trustee and Management Committee: National Occupation Standards* by Workforce Hub (www.ukworkforcehub.org.uk) or the much more substantial book *The Christian Charities Handbook*.

[13] From an article about Jonathan Nelson in *Fortune* magazine (26 May 2008).

[14] Myra & Shelley, *The Leadership Secrets of Billy Graham*, p. 61.

[15] Guinness, *Prophetic Untimeliness*, p. 28.

[16] Guinness, *Prophetic Untimeliness*, p. 15.

[17] Taken from the Buxton Team Parish Magazine, *Speak Out* (June 2008).

Chapter 2: What is that in your hand?

[18] Answering the question of how the research business will develop over the next few years, in *Research* magazine (February 2008): p. 30.

[19] Quoted in: Richard Young, 'Direct Speech', *Research* magazine (February 2008): p. 33.

[20] Beer, *Building a Strategic Church*, p. 23.

[21] Quoted in Guinness, *Prophetic Untimeliness*, p. 17.

[22] Brierley, *Religious Trends* No 7, 2007/2008, table 5.4.

[23] Fleming Drane, *Spirituality to Go*, p. 2.

[24] Full page advertisement in *Fortune* (April 2008).

[25] Taken from the Manfred Kohl Newsletter (March 2007).

[26] Story told in Ross & Carlson, *Say Yes to Your Potential*, p. 31.

[27] Fleming Drane, *Spirituality to Go*, p. 74.

[28] Taken from *Bits and Pieces* 19 (August 1986).

[29] From a talk given by Art Miller, UK CEO Conference, July 1992.

[30] New & Cormack, *Why did I do that?*.

[31] Possible answers might be: Creative – Andrew; Critical – Thomas; Detail – Philip; Resourcer – Andrew; Task – Peter; Team – John; Director – Peter; Shaper – Paul and probably Judas.

[32] Taken from an interview in *Research* magazine (February 2008): p. 47.

Chapter 3: What are you doing here?

[33] Revd John Rockley, Manvers Street Baptist Church, Bath in a leader, *Baptist Times* (5 June 2008).

[34] For example, *Adventures in Tornado Valley*.

[35] From the last verse of the hymn 'Dear Lord and Father of Mankind'.

[36] Erika Lucas, 'Rising above Flood Challenge', *Professional Manager* (March 2008): p. 34.

[37] Article in *The Bookseller* (23 March 1990): p. 943.

[38] Brierley, *Leadership, Vision and Growing Churches*, p. 15.

[39] Much of the rest of this chapter is based on updated excerpts from chapter 2 'I don't have enough time' in *Priorities, Planning and Paperwork*.

[40] Interview with Carl George, 'Behind the Firehouse Syndrome', *Leadership* magazine (Winter 1985): p. 14.

[41] Interview, C. George, *Leadership* magazine.

[42] Interview, C. George, *Leadership* magazine.

[43] MacDonald, *Restoring Your Spiritual Passion*.

[44] Philip D. Harvey & James D. Snyder, 'Charities need a Bottom Line too', *Harvard Business Review* (Jan./Feb. 1987): p.14.

[45] Brierley, *Archdeacons in the early 21st century*, p. 10.

[46] Edward R. Dayton, '"What Next?" Establishing Priorities', *Christian Leadership Letter* (March 1973).

[47] Alan Flavelle, 'The Church – Today and Tomorrow', *Journal of the Irish Christian Study Centre* 2 (1984): p. 28.

[48] John O'Donohue, 'Irish writers and mystics', *Third Way* 31:2 (March 2008): p. 24.

[49] Rush, *Burnout*, p. 13.

[50] Quoted in *Reader's Digest* (August 1990), p. 122.

[51] Sue Walsh quoted in Bryan-Brown, Chloe, 'Find More Time', *Reader's Digest* (November 2007): p. 86.

[52] Dayton, *Tools for Time Management*, p. 51.

[53] Laird & Laird, *The Techniques of Delegating*.

Chapter 4: What do you see?

[54] See, for example, Brierley, *Vision Building*, ch. 3.

[55] Hill, *Flowers in the Cities*.

[56] Naisbitt & Aburdene, *Re-inventing the Corporation*, p. 87.

[57] Townsend, *Mid-Life Crisis*.

[58] Originally spoken in his sermon to the Baptist Association meeting in Northampton, 30 May 1792.

[59] James Williams, 'Utopianism: Dangerous or Essential?', *Engage*19 (from the Jubilee Centre) (Winter 2007): p. 5.

[60] Brierley, *Coming Up Trumps!*, Introduction.

[61] Words taken from Handy, *The Hungry Spirit*, p. 158, describing high quality businesses. The longer quotation is

> There is an abundance of . . . the 'E' factors, energy, enthusiasm, effort, excitement, excellence . . . The talk is about 'we', not 'I', and there is a sense that the

organization is on some sort of crusade, not just to make money, but something grander, something worthy of one's commitment, skills and time.'

[62] *How Not to Have a Pear-Shaped Church*, a Christian Research seminar with Revd Canon David Bracewell, Heather Wraight and Peter Brierley, March 2007.

[63] Much of this detail can also be found at greater length in Brierley, *Coming Up Trumps!*, chs. 4 & 5.

[64] 10 a.m. morning service, 29 June 2003.

[65] Published in *Sigma*, the Eurostat magazine (Summer 1995).

[66] From their advert for a new priest-in-charge, *Church of England Newspaper* (1 February 2008).

[67] Verwer, *Out of the Comfort Zone*, p. 58.

[68] Unknown author, from the prayer letter of Elspeth Aston (February 2008).

[69] Wraight & Wraight, *Back from the Brink*, p. 165.

[70] From Management Future's *Newsletter* (Spring 1996): p. 5 (though they use 'mission' instead of 'vision').

[71] Personal email (15 September 2008) from Don Ford.

[72] *Sheer inspiration*, produced for BT by *Management Today* (2001): p. 11.

[73] Jennie Beck, 'Statement by the Chairman', *MRS News* 11 (May-Jun. 2003): p. 4.

[74] See, for example, the hard-to-read book, Giaquinto, *Visual Thinking in Mathematics*, p. 2.

[75] Extract from letter by CEO Phil Collins, in their *Annual Appeal* (2008): p. 1.

[76] It is dealt with in some detail for example in Brierley, *Coming Up Trumps!*, ch. 4.

[77] From a sermon 'Marching off the map!' by Dr Stan Mooneyham, President of World Vision, 1962–1982, in World Vision's *Prayer Guide* (November/December 2007): p.7.

[78] Chris Neal, Report 'Beyond partnership', Global Connection's *Newsletter* (Autumn 2007): p. 2.

[79] Nicky Gumbel, 'The sign on the bus', *UK Focus* (October 2007): p. 6.

[80] Personal email from the organizer of the original day, July 2008.

[81] John L. Anderson, 'The Horizon Mission Methodology: Modelling and Thinking Within New Paradigms', *Futures Research Quarterly*, (Fall 1995).

[82] Brierley, *Coming Up Trumps!*, p. 117.

[83] Taken from: G. Blake, D. Robinson, & M. Smerdon, *Living Values: A pocket guide for Trustees*, (Community Links, 2006), p. 8. The full report is on www.community-links.org

[84] This is a true story from: Mark Greene, 'Telling tales of truth and transformation', EG 19, (Dec. 2007): p. 8.

[85] For greater detail of such scenarios and others see: Brierley, *Coming Up Trumps!*, ch. 5.

[86] 'The importance of a BHAG', *Next* (May 1997): p. 2.

[87] Ibid.

[88] Brenda Heisenberg, 'Smart Thinking', *The Bookseller* (20 Feb. 2004): p. 22.

[89] From devotions by David Greenlee at the Fifth International Lausanne Researcher's Conference, Australia (April 2008).

[90] Marc Dupont (June 2002).

Chapter 5: Can these dry bones live?

[91] Richard Dannatt, 'Training Leaders to Think Strategically', Christian Research, (May 2002).

[92] Ibid., Page 11.

[93] Brierley, *Church Growth in the 1990s*, Table 22. The actual percentage of churches growing when an Anglican minister has been in the church after 1 or 2 years is 17%; for 3 or 4 years, 17%; for 5 or 6 years, 21%; for 7 to 9 years, 24%; for 10 to 13 years, 22%; for 14 to 17 years, 20%; and for 18 years or longer, 15%.

[94] Quoted in Guinness, *Prophetic Untimeliness*, p. 103.

[95] Discussion paper circulated prior to a Chapter meeting in May 2006.

[96] 'On the right track', *UCL People*, Number 1, June 2008: p. 27.

[97] Jeremy Bullimore, 'What's your problem?', *Management Today* (Mar. 2008): p. 79.

[98] Manfred Kohl, 'Radical change is required for the Leadership of the Church Today', *International Congregational Journal* 6 (2007): p. 114.

[99] Leighton Ford refers to James's leadership as 'outstanding'.

[100] Talk, 'Leadership that can make a positive difference', Peter Kaldor, Fifth International Lausanne Researchers' Conference, Australia, 2008.

[101] 'Author who isn't going to wait for the quiet life', *The Bookseller* (15 Jul. 1994): p. 5.

[102] 'Sonia Gandhi', 'The 100 most influential people in the world', *Time* magazine (12 May 2008): p. 42.

[103] www.managementtoday.co.uk

[104] Morgan, *The Wild Gospel*, p.173.

[105] See, for example: Gary Hamel, 'Management the next move?', *Management Today* (Sept. 2007): p. 53.

[106] Article on 'Careers', *Research* magazine (Dec. 2007): p. 55.

[107] This is the name given to new initiatives being tried by a particular congregation. The phrase comes from the name of an organization started by the current Archbishop of Canterbury, and while it applied initially to new Church of England experiments, the phrase has been taken up by many other denominations. Several thousand examples are listed on the Fresh Expressions website www.freshexpressions.org.uk

[108] Visual Mangalwadi, 'The Key to a New Reformation', *Mission Frontiers* (Mar. 2008): p. 15.

[109] Nelson Mandela, 'The Secrets of Leadership', *Time* magazine (21 Jul. 2008).

[110] Brierley, *Grandparents*, p. 3.

[111] Brierley, *Religious Trends* No 7, 2007/2008, Table 3.3.1.

Reflection: Why wait?

[112] Taken from Overman, *Assumptions that affect our lives*, p. 11.

[113] As given in: Barker, 'Creation: the biblical vision', *Church Times* (5 Sept. 2008), p. 21.

[114] See www.brightsideoflife.co.uk/ethical-framework, William van Dusen Wishard.

[115] Bowen, M., *The Differentiated Self: Essential to Leadership*. Bibliographic details unknown.

[116] J. Oloyede, Glory Bible Church, speaking at Global Connections Conference, The Hayes Conference Centre, Swanwick (28 Nov. 2007).

[117] Revd Derek Hills, Tonbridge Baptist Church (17 Aug. 2008).

[118] Wain, 'Organizational learning and strategic people development', *Research* magazine (Feb. 2008): p. 53.

[119] From *'The Mind Gym: Give me Time*. Part of a selection quoted in 'Your route to the top: How to be humble', *Management Today* (Aug. 2008): p. 15.

[120] MacDonald, *Leadership* magazine (First quarter, 2004): p. 52.

[121] Taken from the 1995 Organizer Pocket Diary.

Chapter 6: Where we are

[122] See T.S. Eliot quoted in the *International Journal of Market Research* 50 (2008): p. 165.

[123] Moynagh & Worsley, *Going Global* (London: A & C Black, 2008).

[124] *The Economist* (3 Nov. 2007).

[125] Jenkins, *The New Faces of Christianity*, p. 153.

[126] Brierley, *Pulling out of the Nosedive*, p. 12.

[127] Horwood, T., *The Future of the Catholic Church in Britain* (London: Laicos Press, 2006).

[128] Bacon, Richard, dissertation analyzing Bristol church closures 1983–2003 (email: MIKEMBacon@aol.com).

[129] Brierley, *The Tide is Running Out.*

[130] Jenkins, *The New Faces of Christianity*, p. 15.

[131] Jonathan Oloyede, 'Black Majority', *Christianity* (Oct. 2005), p. 26.

[132] There are now some 18 new Tamil churches in Britain, for example, doubling their total number.

[133] Cray, *Mission-shaped Church.*

[134] Olson, *The American Church in Crisis*, p. 126.

[135] Measured on at least 10% growth over a nine-year period, in order to give comparisons with figures from 1989 to 1998.

[136] Undertaken on an annual basis by Christian Research since 2001.

[137] Brierley, *Pulling out of the Nosedive*, pp. 129–131, 202.

[138] For example, the number of Roman Catholic baptisms in Scotland, having decreased from 9,100 in 2001 to 7,500 in 2002, increased to 7,600 in 2005, primarily as a result of Polish immigrants working in Glasgow. The Catholic population in the UK went up from 4.0

million in 2003 to 4.3 million in 2005. These figures come from: Brierley, *Religious Trends* No 7, Table 8.14.2.

139 Brierley, *Religious Trends* No 7, Table 4.2.1.

140 Taken from the Church of England website www.cofe.anglican.org/info/statistics/churchstats200 5/statisticspg23.htm (26 Jul. 2008).

141 Number of deaths from Office for National Statistics, *Population Trends* 132 (Summer 2008), Table 2.1; www.cofe.anglican.org; 30% figure based on the proportion of baptisms undertaken by the Church of England and other denominations.

142 Billings, *Secular Lives, Sacred Hearts*, p. 37. This examines the Occasional Offices in detail.

143 Brierley, *Religious Trends* No 7, Table 8.3.1.

144 *Church Growth in the 1990s*. Research report commissioned from Christian Research by Springboard, Oxford, undertaken by P. Brierley (2000).

145 Brierley, *Religious Trends* No 6, Table 5.6.2.

146 Brierley, *Grandparents*, pp. 3, 7.

147 See, for example, Brierley, *Reaching and Keeping Tweenagers* (London: Christian Research, 2002), ch. 1.

148 Idea for Table 6.5b taken from: *Futures* (Spring 2008): p. 6.

149 Speaking at Easter People, Blackpool, 2007.

150 Gavin Peacock, 'On the edge of a goal', *Third Way* (Apr. 2008): p. 13.

151 Standing, *Re-Emerging Church*.

[152] *After McDonaldisation: Mission, Ministry and Christian Discipleship in an Age of Uncertainty*, John Drane, Darton, Longman & Todd, London, April 2008.

[153] Brierley, *Reaching and Keeping Tweenagers*, figure 6.4 & figure 14 and ch. 4.

[154] 'Why young churchgoers ditch church', *Ministry Report* (9 Aug. 2007). See www.ministrytodaymag.com.

[155] Gibbs, E. *Winning Them Back* (Tunbridge Wells: MARC, 1993).

[156] Brierley, P., *Attitudes to Morality and Religion among Secondary School Age Young People*. Christian Research survey report for the Josh McDowell organization (May 2005).

[157] Andrea Wren, 'The next round', *Search* (Spring 2008), Joseph Rowntree Foundation, p. 24. In 1992, 15-year-olds drank an average of 8.1 units a week; in 2006, it was 12.3. However, the greatest acceleration has occurred among 11 to 13-year-olds.

[158] Esther Hughes, 'Why are our young people less happy than they have ever been?', *Church of England Newspaper* (25 Apr. 2008). The Good Childhood Inquiry is managed by The Children's Society.

[159] Statistics taken from www.bstubbs.co.uk/gcse.htm (accessed 15 Sept. 2008) and Peter Brierley, 'The increasing appeal of RS studies', *Church of England Newspaper* (18 Aug. 2008).

[160] Beer, *Building a Strategic Church*, p. 19.

[161] Guinness, *Prophetic Untimeliness*, p. 98.

[162] Brierley, *Religious Trends* No 6, Table 5.5.1.

[163] Brierley, *Religious Trends* No 7, Figure 5.9.8.

164 Brierley, *Religious Trends* No 7, Table 8.2.2.

165 Frost, Wilkinson & Cox, *The Call and the Commission*, ch. 2, table 4.

166 Brierley, *Pulling out of the Nosedive*, p. 179.

167 Morgan, *The Wild Gospel*, p. 191.

168 Park, A., et al (eds), *British Social Attitudes: The 24th Report* (London: National Centre for Social Research & Sage, 2008).

169 Brierley, *Pulling out of the Nosedive*, p. 129.

170 Park et al, *British Social Attitudes: The 24th Report*.

171 ONS, *Population Trends* 132, p. 73.

172 Brierley, *Religious Trends* No 7, table 4.5.4 citing government figures.

173 Brierley, *Attitudes to Morality and Religion.…*

174 Reported on *Newsround* and quoted in Christian Research's *Quadrant* (Sept. 2008), p. 1.

175 Office for National Statistics, *Social Trends* 38 (2008), fig. 4.17.

176 Karen Donnell, *Diversity and different experiences in the UK*, National Statistician's Annual Article on Society, sister publication to *Social Trends* (2008), table 13.

177 ONS, *Population Trends* 132, p. 61.

178 ONS, *Population Trends* 132, p. 51.

179 John Dyson, 'Utopia UK', *Readers' Digest* (Feb. 2006): p.121 (figure from the Countryside Agency).

180 Brierley, *Pulling out of the Nosedive*, table 4.8.

181 James Murphy, 'The Vision', *Research* (Dec. 2007): p. 37.

[182] For example: Taylor, H., *A Toolbox for Small Churches* (Seaford: Thankful Books, 2008).

[183] Jill Bonser, 'We struggle to get to church now', *Woman Alive* (Feb. 2008): p. 39.

[184] Wasdell, D., *Deployment, Growth and Mission in the Church of England* (London: Urban Church Project, 1974).

[185] Thumma & Travis, *Beyond Megachurch Myths*, p. 30.

[186] Olson, *The American Church in Crisis*, p. 57.

[187] Beer, *Building a Strategic Church*, p. 183.

[188] These emerged as *the* key factors in our study, *Leadership, Vision and Growing Churches*, a large-scale survey commissioned by the Salvation Army but across churches of all denominations.

[189] Peter Brierley, *Larger Churches (400+) – an increasingly significant group* (London: Christian Research, 2001). This was a private research report, done from results of focus groups held with those newly joining such.

[190] Brierley, *Larger Churches (400+)*.

[191] Anonymous, 'Church, Families and trying to follow Jesus', *Quadrant* (Sept. 2008), p. 6.

[192] Lesley Garner, 'You can survive the Sandwich Trap', *The Daily Telegraph* (24 Jul. 2007), p. 21.

[193] Diocese of Manchester, *Back to Church Sunday: 26 Sept 2004 Survey Report* (Nov. 2004).

[194] Brierley, *Pulling out of the Nosedive*, ch. 10.

[195] Jason Gardner, 'Hope for Mending the Gap', LICC's *Highlights* (June 2008), p. 2. His book *Mend the Gap* (Nottingham: IVP, 2008) is relevant here.

[196] Gibbs, *Winning Them Back*, p. 299.

[197] Olson, *The American Church in Crisis*, p. 30.

[198] *Evangelicals in the world of the 21st century*, Leaders' Briefing No 21, Peter Brierley, Christian Research, Eltham, London, May 2004, Table 1.

[199] Jenkins, *The New Faces of Christianity*, pp. 184, 187 & 190.

[200] Brierley, *Religious Trends* No 7, table 4.6.

[201] Sookhdeo, *Stepping into the Shadows*, p. 1.

[202] An unpublished calculation.

[203] 'The untold story of Muslims worldwide converting to evangelical Christianity', www.joelrosenberg. blogspot.com (28 Mar. 2008); Laina Farhat-Holtzman, 'Is Islam in Global Flux?', www.familysecurity matters.org (30 Apr. 2008).

[204] Paul-Gordon Chandler, 'Can a Muslim be a Follower of Christ?', *Mission Frontiers* (Jul. 2008): p. 12.

[205] *International Journal of Frontier Missions*, Jan–March and April–June 2007 issues particularly (www.ijfm.org).

[206] Based on numbers given in: Peter Brierley, 'Evangelicals in the world of the 21st century' in *A New Vision, A New Heart and a Renewed Call*, Volume III (ed. David Claydon; Pasadena: William Carey Library, 2005), p. 455.

[207] Ida Glasser, *Trauma, Migration and Mission: Biblical Reflections from a traumatised Hebrew*, Crowther Centre Monographs 2, CMS (Jun. 2008).

[208] *Connections* 7, Numbers 1 & 2 (The Journal of the WEA Mission Commission) (2008).

[209] Figures from: David Barrett, 'Missiometrics 2008', *International Bulletin of Missionary Research* 32, Number 1: pp. 27, 30.

[210] Brierley, *Religious Trends* No 7, Table 2.17.1, etc.

[211] Steven A. Peay (ed.), 'The Church: born for a time like this', *The Fifth Congregational Symposium* 6:2, (Summer 2007), p. 17.

Postscript

[212] *The Wild Gospel*, Alison Morgan, Monarch Books, Oxford UK, 2004, pp. 238, 241.

INDEX

SCRIPTURE INDEX